EXPLORING THE
DA VINCI
CODE

Other Resources by Lee Strobel and Garry Poole

Discussing the Da Vinci Code

Experiencing the Passion of Jesus

Faith Under Fire 1, Faith and Jesus
(participant's guide, DVD, and leader's guide)

Faith Under Fire 2, Faith and Facts
(participant's guide, DVD, and leader's guide)

Faith Under Fire 3, Tough Faith Questions
(participant's guide, DVD, and leader's guide)

Faith Under Fire 4, A New Kind of Faith
(participant's guide, DVD, and leader's guide)

Other Resources by Lee Strobel

The Case for Christ

The Case for Christ audio

The Case for Christ—Student Edition (with Jane Vogel)

The Case for Christmas

The Case for a Creator

The Case for a Creator audio

The Case for a Creator—Student Edition (with Jane Vogel)

The Case for Easter

The Case for Faith

The Case for Faith audio

The Case for Faith—Student Edition (with Jane Vogel)

God's Outrageous Claims

Inside the Mind of Unchurched Harry and Mary

Surviving a Spiritual Mismatch in Marriage (with Leslie Strobel)

Surviving a Spiritual Mismatch in Marriage audio

What Jesus Would Say

Other Resources by Garry Poole

The Complete Book of Questions

Seeker Small Groups

The Three Habits of Highly Contagious Christians

In the Tough Questions Series:

Don't All Religions Lead to God?

How Could God Allow Suffering and Evil?

How Does Anyone Know God Exists?

Why Become a Christian?

Tough Questions Leader's Guide (with Judson Poling)

INVESTIGATING THE ISSUES RAISED BY THE BOOK & MOVIE

EXPLORING THE
DA VINCI
CODE

LEE
STROBEL

GARRY
POOLE

ZONDERVAN™

GRAND RAPIDS, MICHIGAN 49530 USA

ZONDERVAN.COM/
AUTHORTRACKER

We want to hear from you. Please send your
comments about this book to us in care of
zreview@zondervan.com. Thank you.

ZONDERVAN™

Exploring the Da Vinci Code
Copyright © 2006 by Lee Strobel and Garry Poole

Requests for information should be addressed to:

Zondervan, *Grand Rapids, Michigan 49530*

ISBN-10: 0-310-27372-2
ISBN-13: 978-0-310-27372-1

Interior design by Beth Shagene

Printed in the United States of America

06 07 08 09 10 11 • 15 14 13 12 11 10 9 8 7 6 5 4 3 2 1

CONTENTS

ABOUT THE AUTHORS

Lee Strobel

Atheist-turned-Christian Lee Strobel is the bestselling author of nearly twenty books, including the award-winners *The Case for Christ*, *The Case for Faith*, and *The Case for a Creator*. With a Master of Studies in Law degree from Yale Law School, he was a journalist at the *Chicago Tribune* and elsewhere, winning Illinois' top honors for investigative reporting (shared with a team he led) and public service journalism from United Press International. He and his wife live in California.

Garry Poole

Garry Poole, director of spiritual discovery at Willow Creek Community Church in suburban Chicago, is a leading innovator of small groups designed to help spiritual seekers investigate Christianity. His award-winning book *Seeker Small Groups* provides a blueprint for implementing this highly successful ministry. Garry also authored *The Complete Book of Questions* and the bestselling Tough Questions series. He and Lee Strobel wrote *Experiencing the Passion of Jesus*, named the 2005 Christian Book of the Year. Garry lives outside Chicago.

INTRODUCTION

Actual conversation on an airplane over Iowa:

Passenger 1: You're a Christian too? So am I. That's great.

Passenger 2: Yeah, that's great.

(pause)

Passenger 1: I just read *The Da Vinci Code*. Have you read it?

Passenger 2: Sure did.

Passenger 1: What percentage do you think is true?

(pause)

Passenger 2: Oh, about 80 percent.

Dan Brown's red-hot page-turner *The Da Vinci Code* has become a runaway bestseller and now a major motion picture directed by Ron Howard. What's most intriguing, though, is not merely the astronomical sales figures—it's the effect the story is having on popular culture. By cleverly mixing fact with fiction, Brown has created a raging controversy over how many of the novel's claims are rooted in reality.

USA Today said the book consists of "historical fact with a contemporary storyline." Said Charles Taylor of the popular website *salon.com*: "The most amazing thing about this novel is that it's based on fact." Brown even begins his book under the heading "FACT," telling his readers: "All descriptions of artwork, architecture, documents, and secret rituals in this novel are accurate."

If true, the book's assertions are nothing less than breathtaking: Jesus never claimed to be the Son of God but was actually deified nearly three hundred years later by Emperor Constantine for his own nefarious purposes; Jesus was married to Mary Magdalene, who bore his child; Jesus wanted Mary Magdalene to lead his church, but she was forced out by power-hungry men and demonized as a prostitute; and the four Gospels in the Bible are essentially fabrications designed to seal this masculine power-grab for the rest of history.

Are readers being convinced? A survey by Decima Research, Inc. showed that one out of three Canadians who have read the book now believes there are descendants of Jesus walking among us today. And according to pollster George Barna, 53 percent of Americans who've read the book said it had been helpful in their "personal spiritual growth and understanding." But are *The Da Vinci Code's* stunning allegations actually supported by the historical evidence? Or are they as fanciful as the novel's colorful characters?

To get answers, my colleague Garry Poole and I traveled to France to visit the Musée du Louvre, between the Seine River and the Rue de Rivoli, in the heart of Paris. This magnificent museum, once the luxurious Renaissance palace of Louis XIV, houses thousands of paintings by Rembrandt, Rubens, Poussin, and others, as well as such sculptures as the Winged Victory of Samothrace and the Venus de Milo.

The Da Vinci Code begins with the murder of the Louvre's fictional curator, Jacques Saunière, whose body is found thirty yards from Leonardo Da Vinci's painting, *Mona Lisa*. Clever codes and clues lead Harvard professor

Robert Langdon (played by Academy Award winner Tom Hanks in the movie) and the curator's granddaughter, Sophie Neveu (played by Audrey Tauton), on a whirlwind adventure of discovery.

As part of our investigation, Garry and I examined architect I. M. Pei's impressive glass pyramid that was added to the Louvre in 1989—under which, according to the closing pages of *The Da Vinci Code*, are buried the bones of Mary Magdalene and a cache of ancient documents about her true identity. Through the centuries, the church has allegedly done everything in its power to cover up the explosive truth about her and suppress the female role in Christianity.

We also went to England to explore other key sites from *The Da Vinci Code*, such as the Temple Church in London. This striking medieval edifice, with eerie stone effigies of nine knights embedded in its circular foyer, was built by the Knights Templar, the part-military, part-religious organization that Brown claims was the protector of the secrets about Jesus and Mary Magdalene.

Before virtually all of the Knights Templar were slain centuries ago, their task of passing down these secrets was entrusted, Brown claims, to the Priory of Sion, a clandestine organization supposedly founded by a descendant of Jesus in 1099. Among the Priory's purported Grand Masters: Sir Isaac Newton, Victor Hugo—and Leonardo Da Vinci, who allegedly left clues in some of his most famous artwork.

Frankly, Garry and I found the process of examining the claims of *The Da Vinci Code* every bit as fascinating as the murder mystery itself. And we're glad that you too want to get to the bottom of the important issues raised by Brown, especially these four fundamental questions:

- What can history really tell us?
- Can we trust the four Gospels?
- What's the role of women in Christianity?
- Is Jesus the Son of God?

In this book, you'll read the interviews we conducted with four recognized scholars who are experts in ancient history, the Gospels, women in Christianity, and the deity of Jesus. We've also included provocative quotes and sidebars on related issues, as well as a series of questions that we hope will stimulate your thinking or provide fodder for your conversations with friends. (We've created a separate DVD-driven resource called *Discussing the Da Vinci Code* if you'd like to get together with a few others to talk about the book and movie.) At the conclusion of each chapter, I'll offer my own perspective.

When I was an atheist and began my probe into the case for Christianity, I promised myself that I would maintain an open mind and follow the facts wherever they lead—and I hope you'll make that same resolution as you begin your journey into exploring this controversial book and film. In the end, I trust you'll come to your own well-reasoned conclusions about the claims of *The Da Vinci Code*.

The truth is, there is a lot at stake: can Jesus really be trusted as God incarnate, or was he merely a human pawn in the greatest scam in history? So engage, analyze, study, deliberate, grow—and then decide for yourself.

Have a great time exploring *The Da Vinci Code*!

Lee Strobel

Chapter 1

WHAT CAN HISTORY REALLY TELL US?

Blinding ignorance does mislead us.
O! Wretched mortals, open your eyes!
Leonardo da Vinci

Breathtaking Lincoln Cathedral, towering atop Lindum Hill in a quaint community two hours by train north of London, can be seen from twenty miles away. Some say it's among the finest medieval buildings in all of Europe. Its edifice, parts of which date back to 1072, is awash in spotlights at night, creating a spectacular golden glow.

I pulled open the massive black door and walked inside. The cavernous sanctuary, with its arched ceilings and elegant stained glass, still functions as a church today. Exploring a long hallway, our footsteps echoing as we went, Garry and I came upon a small room to the right and opened the door, which creaked eerily on its hinges. Our eyes immediately were captured by an elegant statue along the wall—a finely carved marble image of a winged

11

and bearded figure bearing a written proclamation. How ancient was it? Fifteenth century? Earlier?

I smiled and picked it up, easily holding it above my head. "Look!" I exclaimed. "Styrofoam!"

Sure enough, the statue was a clever fake. Next to it was a monument that purported to date back centuries— but it was made of plywood. And the stone wall with beautiful frescos painted on it? The whole thing was drawn on heavy canvas—including the stones themselves.

Ron Howard had been here.

As director of *The Da Vinci Code* movie, he had been faced with a challenge. The plot of the book climaxes with a confrontation at London's Westminster Abbey, but officials there refused to let Howard film his movie inside their historic walls. The reason, they said, is that the novel is filled with "factual errors" and was "theologically unsound."

So Howard went hunting for another ancient building that could pass for the interior of the 940-year-old Abbey. That brought him to Lincoln Cathedral.

Cathedral officials were critical of Brown's book too, calling it "speculative and far-fetched," and even heretical in places, "based on ideas put forward rather late in the church's history." Still, they opted to open their doors for the filming of three of the movie's scenes. "The book claims that the church has suppressed important facts about Jesus," the Cathedral's dean said in a statement. "The way to counter this accusation is to be open about the facts as we understand them and welcome vigorous debate."

Once inside, Hollywood did what it does best: create illusions. Phony paintings, crypts, and statues were skillfully designed and constructed. To the casual observer, they appeared every bit as real as the other historic artifacts in the medieval cathedral. On camera, they would undoubtedly fool viewers.

In a way, this harmless Hollywood trickery is a metaphor for the more insidious illusions that, according to Dan Brown, have fooled students of history for generations. His basic charge in *The Da Vinci Code* is that people have been misled and deceived by historical accounts about Jesus that have no basis in reality. History, Brown asserts, is written by the winners, who naturally paint themselves in positive ways while disparaging their defeated foes—and so we're left with a biased and tainted record that only tells one side of the story.

"Almost everything our fathers taught us about Christ," says a character in the novel, "is *false*."

What *can* we know for sure about history? How can we assess whether an ancient document is trustworthy? Are there legitimate criteria we can use to test historical claims? And what about some of the eye-popping historical allegations that Brown makes, such as his assertion that the Priory of Sion has been protecting the secrets about Jesus, Mary Magdalene, and their descendants for centuries? Or that it was Emperor Constantine, an ersatz Christian, who deified Jesus, collated the Bible, and destroyed competing gospels in order to eliminate the real story about Jesus' identity?

I placed a call to Dr. Paul Maier, a well-respected and straight-shooting professor of ancient history, and made an appointment to question him about these issues. It was time to get some answers.

1. What was your overall reaction to *The Da Vinci Code*? What are three things you liked most about the book or movie? What did you like least — and why?

2. Are there any questions, issues, or concerns about historical Christianity that *The Da Vinci Code* raises in your mind? If so, what are they specifically?

Gauging Historical Accuracy

"Many historians now believe (as do I) that in gauging the historical accuracy of a given concept, we should first ask ourselves a far deeper question: How historically accurate is history itself?"

Dan Brown

3. Can historical events be verified? Why or why not? What do you think determines whether or not a historical event actually occurred?

Dr. Maier, a wiry and feisty professor of ancient history at Western Michigan University, has achieved acclaim as a scholar, teacher, and author of both academic and popular writings. Since earning his doctorate at the University of

Basel in Switzerland in 1957, he has become a recognized expert on ancient Near East history, ancient Greek and Roman history, and Christianity and the Roman Empire. He has written more than 250 articles and reviews for professional journals, including the *Harvard Theological Review*. His teaching awards include Professor of the Year from the Council for the Advancement and Support of Education.

Maier has written such books as *In the Fullness of Time*, which examines secular evidence about Jesus and early Christianity; a new translation and commentary on the first-century historian Josephus; and a similar book on Eusebius, the first church historian. He's also the author of historical novels, including *Pontius Pilate* and *The Flames of Rome*. His thriller *A Skeleton in God's Closet* became the top national bestseller in religious fiction and led to a sequel, *More Than a Skeleton*.

Maier has more than just a passing interest in *The Da Vinci Code*. Together with Hank Hanegraaff, host of the popular national radio program *The Bible Answer Man*, he conducted an in-depth analysis of Brown's novel. From that research, he and Hanegraaff wrote *The Da Vinci Code: Fact or Fiction?*, which provides answers to historical issues raised by the book.

When we rendezvoused in California, sitting across from each other in a borrowed room, I opened my copy of *The Da Vinci Code* and read aloud this quote: "History is always written by the winners. When two cultures clash, the loser is obliterated and the winner writes the history books—books which glorify their own cause and disparage the conquered foe."

I looked up at Maier. "Do you agree with that?" I asked. "Is history always written by the winners?"

Maier didn't hesitate. "No, the whole premise is false," he declared. "I can give you some interesting instances where history was written by the losers. For example, one of the greatest civil wars in the ancient world was the famous Peloponnesian War. [Its history] was written by Thucydides, who was an Athenian, and the Athenians lost the war. Sparta won. And yet, Thucydides wrote a very objective treatment of what happened in the Peloponnesian War."

With that quick refutation of one of Brown's major premises, our conversation continued to unfold:

Q: What determines whether a historical event actually occurred? How do you know, as a historian, that any event in ancient history really took place?

Maier: There are various methods. First of all, "multiple attestations," or different authors writing about the same event, is one criteria for authenticity. For example, we have three different versions of the great fire of Rome in 64 AD. Basically, all three of them attest that Rome was totally destroyed, or at least that Rome was only partially destroyed, so this does not deny that the great fire of Rome actually happened. We know it did happen.

Q: So there might be some differences in secondary details, but the core is trustworthy because you have multiple reports on the same event?

Maier: Exactly. Another interesting criterion is the "criterion of embarrassment." In other words, very often we can bring more truth out of a hostile source than a friendly one. A friendly source can beef up or exaggerate its particular role, but when a hostile source concedes something because everybody knows it really occurred, then the ancient historian concludes that's the truth.

There are other methods of determining the truth behind historical events as well. Archaeologists give us hard evidence that sheds light on a particular source, like geographical data and background. If the setting of the event is accurate and one can go see it today, we know it's true. Flavius Josephus, the famous first-century Jewish historian, talks about the siege of Masada. Well, you can go to Masada today and see the very snake path that he talked about two thousand years ago on the east side of that great crag. This confirms that Josephus was not just making this up.

Q: But as a Christian, doesn't that bias your view of history?

Maier: I try the best I possibly can to be objective in historical research. I think every true historian is digging for the truth. In the case of archaeology or ancient historical research, we look for the truth and let the chips fall where they may. And what is so incredibly interesting about the chips in the case of Christianity is how they fall on the side of supporting the biblical record.

Q: What about the bias of the person in ancient history who is doing the reporting? You mentioned that Josephus was a Jewish historian of the first century. He certainly had his biases. How do you sort through that as a historian?

Maier: You've got to learn to put on filters. For example, we know that Josephus in the *War of the Jews* was very partisan to the Roman side and he tries to favor his own benefactors in Rome. So we must neutralize that somewhat in reverse against his admiration for things Roman. Now, later on, he's a little more honest when he does the *Antiquities*. And so, you always try to check out the source's bias, and then put a reverse negative filter on that to get at the truth.

Maier's basic point—that historians use sensible and proven approaches to figure out what really happened in ancient times—did make sense to me. I was particularly fascinated by his comment about how these approaches tend to support the biblical record—but I knew I'd be delving deeper into this topic in future interviews. In the meantime, I turned our conversation to a historical claim by Brown that a clandestine organization called the Priory of Sion has spent centuries guarding the secret about the descendants of Jesus. I was curious about how well this assertion would withstand a historian's scrutiny.

"The book makes the claim that this information about the Priory is contained in secret documents that were discovered in the National French Library," I said. "Would you not concede that those documents do exist?"

Clearly, I had struck a nerve. "The documents exist—but they're all fraudulent!" Maier exclaimed. "On the first page of *The Da Vinci Code*, Dan Brown lists two items as 'FACT': Opus Dei and the Priory of Sion. Now, this is his method. He will offer a little truth—maybe 15 to 20 percent—and the rest is falsehood. But people will think it's all true because they know that part of it is true. The claim in *The Da Vinci Code* is that the Priory of Sion was founded in 1099 AD in Jerusalem. Well, the fact of the matter is that it was founded in 1956, in Paris, by a crook and forger named Pierre Plantard, who planted secret documents in the Bibliothèque Nationale in Paris."

Maier was gravely offended by the notion. "The central strand in *The DaVinci Code* is based on fraud," he said. "This is just incredible!"

Indeed, it *was* amazing! "So the documents are real; the problem is that they're phony," I said.

"They're *totally* phony!" he replied. "Exactly!"

Suddenly, it was as if a crucial thread had been pulled out of *The Da Vinci Code* and its central premise began to unravel. So many of its allegations, including the supposed involvement of Leonardo Da Vinci as a Grand Master of the Priory, can be traced back to counterfeit documents that have absolutely no basis in reality. And with the claims about the Priory being so confidently labeled as "fact" by Brown, what repercussions does this have for the overall credibility of his work?

"When you see this as a historian," I asked Maier, "what does that do to you?"

"Well, I worry about the truth. I really do," Maier replied. "What happens if a majority of the readers of this novel will believe all the lies that are included in the second half of the book? Will this become the majority opinion? And will those historians who are really seeking the truth be crowded out in the future?

"Actually, I am far more furious at *The Da Vinci Code* as a professor of ancient history than I am as a Christian. The church has been attacked for two thousand years now. Well, what's new? But I cannot stand it when universally accepted facts of the past are falsified. This I cannot take."

Then he gave the ultimate insult a college professor can offer. "If a student of mine had written something like this," he declared, "I would flunk him!"

4. What's your reaction to Dr. Maier's revelation about the Priory of Sion? Do you think he's being too harsh by saying he would have given Brown an "F" if he had been a student? Why?

5. Dan Brown's statements about the Priory of Sion are listed under the bold headline, "FACT." What does this suggest about the accuracy of the rest of the book's claims? Explain.

Dan Brown: A Believer

"I began as a skeptic. As I started researching *Da Vinci Code*, I really thought I would disprove a lot of this theory about Mary Magdalene and holy blood and all of that. I became a believer."

**Dan Brown to Elizabeth Vargas
on ABC's *Primetime Live***

Error-Laden?

"So error-laden is *The Da Vinci Code* that the educated reader actually applauds those rare occasions where Brown stumbles (despite himself) into the truth."

Sandra Miesel in *Crisis* magazine

6. Generally speaking, what percentage of Dan Brown's book do you think is fact and what percentage of it is fiction?

The Priory of Sion

"Brown relies on a 1982 publication, *Holy Blood, Holy Grail*, for his information on the Priory of Sion. The authors of *Holy Blood, Holy Grail* relied on documents provided them by Pierre Plantard, who spent time in jail for fraud in 1953. Plantard and three other men started a small social club in 1956 called the Priory of Sion.... Throughout the 1960s and the 1970s, Plantard created a series of documents 'proving' the existence of a bloodline descending from Mary Magdalene, through the kings of France, down to the present day to include (surprise!) Pierre Plantard.... In 1993 ... Plantard, under oath, admitted he had made up the whole Priory scheme."

James Garlow and Peter Jones
in *Cracking Da Vinci's Code*

7. Listed below are some of *The Da Vinci Code*'s controversial claims that are disputed by numerous historians and biblical scholars. To what extent do you think people view these controversial theories as factual? Generally speaking, what's your opinion about these theories? Check any that you consider to be accurate.

☐ The Bible was put together by Constantine, a pagan Roman emperor.

☐ The Gospels have been edited to support the claims of later Christians.

- [ ] Jesus is not the Son of God; he was only a man.
- [ ] Jesus was not viewed as God until the fourth century, when he was deified by the Emperor Constantine.
- [ ] Jesus was married to Mary Magdalene.
- [ ] In the original Gospels, Mary Magdalene, not Peter, was directed to establish the church.
- [ ] Mary Magdalene was to be worshiped as a goddess.
- [ ] There is a secret society known as the Priory of Sion that still worships Mary Magdalene as a goddess and is trying to keep that practice alive.
- [ ] Jesus and Mary Magdalene conceived a child and named her Sarah.
- [ ] Sarah gave rise to a prominent family line that is still present in Europe today.
- [ ] The Catholic Church often has assassinated the descendants of Christ to keep his bloodline from growing.

Trustworthy?

"*The Da Vinci Code* clearly contains many historical errors covering a wide variety of issues: church architecture, religious symbolism, the Roman Empire, ancient Israel, and different spiritual belief systems. If Brown cannot be relied upon to accurately recount the most basic of historical facts, then how can he be trusted to correctly explain more complex subjects?"

Richard Abanes in
The Truth Behind the Da Vinci Code

8. Do you think that Christianity, as we know it, is a fabrication, and that the truth has been repressed?

History Mixed with Falsehoods

"This is a good airplane book, a novelistic thriller that presents a rummage sale of accurate historical nuggets alongside falsehoods and misleading statements. The bottom line: The book should come coded for 'black light,' like the pen used by the character Saunière to record his dying words so that readers could scan pages to see which 'facts' are trustworthy and which patently not."

Margaret M. Mitchell, chair of the Department of New Testament and Early Christian Literature at the University of Chicago

One of the villains in *The Da Vinci Code* is the Roman emperor, Constantine. Brown called him a pagan who only reluctantly converted to Christianity on his death-bed and who decided which gospels went into the Bible and which were destroyed because they revealed that Jesus was a mere human being. Obviously, these weighty claims are worth investigating, so I continued my inter-view with Dr. Maier by summarizing Brown's assertions and then saying, "You're a historian—is this historically reliable information?"

Again, Maier was incensed at the very suggestion. "I think it's the greatest character assassination I've ever seen —either fact or fiction—in my life," he insisted. "This flies flat in the face of all the historical evidence we have.

"Constantine was a true convert to Christianity. After the Battle of Milvian Bridge, he announced the Edict of Toleration for the faith. He built cathedrals as though there were no tomorrow. All the main identification spots associated with Jesus in Palestine are Constantinian construction: the Church of the Nativity in Bethlehem and the Church of the Holy Sepulcher in Jerusalem.

"He couldn't do enough for the church. He reimbursed the church for all the damage it had suffered in the persecutions. He invited the clergy regularly for dinner. He called himself a bishop of those outside the church in order to bring them into the church. He felt that God had appointed him to convert the Roman Empire to Christianity. He was active in church affairs. He exempted the clergy from taxation. He called the first great ecumenical council into session—and I could go on. It's ridiculous to say he was a lifelong pagan. It's simply a bald lie."

I thought to myself, *Tell me how you really feel, Dr. Maier. Next time, don't hold back!* Clearly, as a historian he was angry about what he considers the blatant defamation of Constantine. "But," I interjected, "is it true that Constantine is the one who collated the Bible, and that he chose what gospels went in and which got eliminated?"

Maier wasn't buying that either. "Dan Brown almost makes Constantine a universal editor of the earliest Bible, which is just pathetic, because the canon [the standard biblical books] was already known a century and a half to two hundred years before Constantine. Eusebius, the earliest Christian church historian, tells us how the canon came to be and how other books were added later on, but by Constantine's time, it was already determined. There's no question about that.

"And the Council of Nicea in 325 did not decide which books should go in the canon or which should not. Nothing of that is true. Not one of the decrees of the Council of Nicea deals with the canon. So, again, you simply have falsehood multiplied here."

I asked Maier about another *DaVinci Code* claim: that Constantine used the Council of Nicea to deify Jesus in AD 325.

"Well, this is what Dan Brown says," Maier replied. "But the deity of Jesus was never under discussion at the Council of Nicea. What was under discussion was whether Jesus was coeternal with the Father or not. And this is what was decided."

Maier anticipated my follow-up question. "By the way," he concluded, "Dan Brown says it was a very close vote. Well, let me tell you what the close vote was: about 300 to 2. Not too close, as far as I can tell."

I asked, "If you could sum up in one word how reliable *The Da Vinci Code* is in terms of reporting on what Constantine did, what would that one word be?"

Maier didn't heed my word limit, but he made his point clear. "I would say 20 percent truth, 80 percent falsehood," he said. "That's more than one word, but that sums it up."

9. How convincing was Dr. Maier in rebutting Brown's allegations about Emperor Constantine? Has he caused you to doubt the veracity of Brown's claims? Why or why not?

10. If there are so many fallacies contained within *The Da Vinci Code*, why do you think so many people accept the book as a story based on facts and actual historical events?

11. Do you think Dan Brown had an agenda in writing his book, *The Da Vinci Code*? Why or why not? If so, what do you think it was?

It Didn't Happen?

"Brown claims that Jesus wanted the movement that followed him to be about a greater awareness of the 'sacred feminine.' He says that this movement, under the leadership and inspiration of Mary Magdalene, thrived during the first three centuries until it was brutally suppressed by the Emperor Constantine. *There's no evidence to suggest that this is true. It didn't happen.*"

Historian Amy Welborn in *De-Coding Da Vinci*

Since Dr. Maier is not only a historian but also a best-selling novelist, I thought it would be interesting to ask his opinion of how Brown approached the writing of *The Da Vinci Code*. Catholic historian Amy Welborn, in her book *De-Coding Da Vinci*, suggests that writers of historical fiction make an implicit deal with their readers—that while the novel features fictional characters engaged in imagined activities, the basic historical framework is itself correct. But in *The Da Vinci Code*, she said, fanciful details and false historical assertions are presented as facts and the product of serious historical research. I wanted to know: is that a legitimate way to craft a novel?

"You wrote a wonderful book called *Pontius Pilate*, and you were careful to maintain the accuracy of the background facts and events, but then you felt the freedom to create a story in the forefront," I said to Maier. "But what Dan Brown seems to have done is not maintain the historic foundation for his book. Is that right?"

"Oh, yes, indeed," Maier said. "In the case of both my historical works, *Pontius Pilate* and *The Flames of Rome*, I was extremely careful. Every personality in the books really lived, and I used their actual names. Secondly, I never contradict known historical facts. Only where the facts leave off do I then try to provide fictional mortar to hold the story together. And I'll own up with the reader at the end of the book. This is in total contrast to what Dan Brown did."

"But that's just a different approach, isn't it?" I asked. "Does that mean Brown's approach is wrong?"

"Well, Brown's approach is wrong simply because he lies about the facts," said Maier. "And you dare not lie about known historical facts."

Still, were we making too much of a book that is quite appropriately shelved under "fiction" at Barnes & Noble? I pointed out to Maier that some people scoff at his concerns, saying, "Come on, Dr. Maier, it's just a novel. Would you just lighten up? Dan Brown wrote a good story, he had fun with it, and people enjoy reading it. Why do you get so upset about a mere novel?"

"What would you say to that?" I asked.

"I get this a lot—'Come on! Chill out, Maier! It's a novel!' And that's a valid challenge," he began. "The answer is simply this: in a novel, you have foreground characters and you have the background setting. Now, the foreground characters—you can do with them as you wish. I would never criticize Dan Brown for whatever he might want to do with his fictional characters. That's his privilege as a novelist, and I'm not knocking that at all.

"But the setting and the background that are well-known from history should not be tampered with, in the interest of credibility. Have there been any novels written about World War II? Of course there have. Well, in every one of those novels, you have foreground characters who are fictional—they never lived, and so forth—but in the background—surprise! surprise!—the Allies always win and the Nazis always lose, don't they? Why? Because that's what happened.

"Now, what Dan Brown has done is to fictionalize his foreground characters. Fine—have at it! But in the process he has also falsified the background, and that is what is absolutely unacceptable. In other words, if Dan Brown were using the same rules that he used for *The Da Vinci Code* to write a novel about World War II, he would have Hitler winning the war and Roosevelt on trial in Washington, D.C., and Churchill on trial in London. That's how bad it is.

"And people who don't know history—who aren't aware of the past—might think, 'Wow, what do you know? That must have happened. It's in print!' That's the danger."

Indeed, I thought to myself as I concluded our conversation, the biggest problem with *The Da Vinci Code* is that many of its readers simply aren't sufficiently conversant with ancient history to recognize the blatant inaccuracies that plague the book.

12. Some people assert that *The Da Vinci Code* is just a novel with no harm done. Others have a problem with the way the book is portrayed as a fact-based exposé that purports to teach history and reveal truths within the framework of fiction. In your opinion, is *The Da Vinci Code* just a novel with no harm done or is it cause for alarm? Why?

13. In the *National Review*, David Klinghoffer wrote, "What's at stake in *The Da Vinci Code* is nothing less than traditional Christianity itself." Do you think that *The Da Vinci Code* poses any real threat to Christianity? Why or why not?

While in England to investigate the sites featured in *The Da Vinci Code*, Garry and I ventured to historic Highgate Cemetery in North London, once a fashionable burial place for members of Victorian society. One of history's greatest scientists, Michael Faraday, is among the 52,000 people buried there.

We walked down the muddy, leaf-strewn pathway during a typical British drizzle, straining to read the inscriptions on the tombstones, until we eventually came upon paved sidewalks in the more modern section of the thirty-seven-acre estate. Suddenly, we encountered the grave of Karl Marx. The stern-looking father of communism is depicted in an impressive, larger-than-life bust atop his monument. As we were getting ready to take some souvenir photos, a cemetery worker quickly cleaned off some mud that had apparently been thrown at the monument by a passing capitalist.

As I read the monument's inscription, I was struck by a particular phrase: "The philosophers have only interpreted the world in various ways...." Is it really true that history is always based on someone's interpretation—or are there some events that we can know for a fact?

Every trial I've covered as a legal journalist investigated an event of recent history. Did the defendant murder the victim? Did the doctor commit malpractice? To determine the truth, jurors consider eyewitness testimony, study documents, and examine physical evidence—and in the end, they reach a verdict.

In a way, the study of ancient evidence is similar. Do we have records that are rooted in eyewitness accounts and are close to the events themselves? Does archaeology corroborate or contradict the testimony? By carefully examining the evidence and employing the kind of investigative criteria described by Dr. Maier, we can come to a reasonable verdict about whether an event occurred long ago.

When I apply those standards to the historical claims of *The Da Vinci Code*, I walk away totally unconvinced that they're based on reality. They simply do not hold up to sober scrutiny. The Priory of Sion? Sorry, its thousand-year legacy of passing along the secrets about Jesus and Mary Magdalene is simply mythology created by counterfeit documents. Emperor Constantine? There are just too many historically reliable records that contradict Brown's fanciful reconstruction of history.

But what about the Gospels in the New Testament? Do they only provide a distorted and unreliable record about Jesus, as Brown contends? Or is there solid evidence that they are trustworthy accounts of Christ's birth, teachings, miracles, death, and resurrection? That would be my next topic to tackle. It was time to find a Jesus scholar to see if he could back up his claims with facts.

Chapter 2

CAN WE TRUST
THE FOUR GOSPELS?

Many have made a trade of delusions
and false miracles, deceiving the stupid multitude.
Leonardo da Vinci

It was a subtle scent that first captivated me as I walked
through the doorway into the library at Lincoln Cathedral. *Old leather. Aged parchments.* Then as I stepped into
the narrow room, I saw a wall of shelves that were filled,
top to bottom, with hundreds upon hundreds of written
treasures—dark-bound ancient books and manuscripts,
each one of them brimming with history.

Among them was a collection of sermons by the Venerable Bede, the father of English history, dating back
almost one thousand years. This scholar-monk, who
authored or translated more than forty books, wrote
the first historical work that used the BC/AD dating
system. Then there was one of four remaining copies of
the Magna Carta from 1215, which limited the power of

British monarchs and was a crucial step toward constitutional law. There was even a schoolbook from 1410 that contained the first recorded rhyme about the legendary Robin Hood from Sherwood Forest in the nearby county of Nottinghamshire.

Our journey to Lincoln Cathedral, where actors Tom Hanks and Audrey Tauton played out scenes for *The Da Vinci Code* movie, was taking me much further back into history than I had anticipated. Entering this library filled with invaluable tomes prompted an important question: how reliable are the historical documents that tell us about what happened in long-ago times?

For instance, when the Venerable Bede wrote his classic five-part history of England, the *Historia ecclesiastica gentis Anglorum*, was he providing reliable information or spinning an imaginative but convincing tale? As a scholar, Bede was careful to meticulously document his sources—and he was quite concerned about where those sources got their information. He sought out oral testimony about more recent historic events, and he even invented the practice of footnoting. But in the end, can we trust what he wrote?

In a similar way, can we trust what the New Testament tells us about the life, death, and resurrection of Jesus? Not according to *The Da Vinci Code*. Sir Leigh Teabing (played by Ian McKellen in the movie), the symbologist who lectures the naive Sophie on the "real" story about Christianity, dismisses the Gospels as skewed and biased reports that inaccurately claim Jesus was the unique Son of God. Until the Council of Nicea in 325, he said, "Jesus was viewed by his followers as a mortal prophet ... a great and powerful man, but a *man* nonetheless." Dozens of competing gospels that described Jesus as merely human, he said, were systematically excluded from the Bible by Emperor Constantine.

Is that version of history true? Was the other side of Jesus' story banned from the Bible in an effort to fool people into thinking he was divine? Or are there solid historical reasons for trusting the four Gospels in the Bible?

In a search for a credible source who can analyze these issues, I contacted Dr. Scot McKnight, a formidable scholar who specializes in historical Jesus studies and the Gospels — and who, incidentally, earned his doctorate at the University of Nottingham in Robin Hood's old stomping grounds not too far from the Lincoln Cathedral.

1. Growing up, what do you remember hearing or believing about the Bible? Did you readily believe what you were told, or did you tend to be skeptical about its contents?

Faith and Metaphors

"Every religion describes God through metaphor, allegory, and exaggeration, from the early Egyptians through modern Sunday school.... The problems arise when we begin to believe literally in our own metaphors."

The Da Vinci Code

2. Select the statement(s) that best describe your current view of the Bible. What are some reasons that support your view?

☐ The Bible has no relevance for me.

☐ The Bible is an interesting religious book, but it is a mixture of human truth and human error.

☐ The Bible is no different from other writings that claim to come from God.

☐ The Bible has remarkable wisdom, but that doesn't mean it's God's Word.

☐ The Bible has a lot of value and God works through it, but that doesn't mean it's the only book God uses.

☐ The Bible is inspired by God, but not the only book inspired by him.

☐ The Bible contains God's truths, yet not everything in it is from God.

☐ The Bible—all of it, and only it—is God's Word through the words of men.

☐ Other: _____

Dr. Scot McKnight was visiting California when we sat down for an interview in the office of a friend of mine at Biola University. McKnight, balding and bespectacled, a former college basketball player who has now taken up the more genteel game of golf, is often sought after by journalists who are investigating historical issues about Jesus or the New Testament. It's not unusual to see him quoted in *U.S. News & World Report, Time, Newsweek,* or on national network television.

McKnight has been a professor of religious studies at Chicago's North Park University for more than a decade. He has authored more than ten books and contributed to numerous others, including one of my favorites, *Jesus Under Fire*. His first book, *Interpreting the Synoptic Gospels*, has been in print for more than fifteen years. He is editor or coeditor of *The Dictionary of Jesus and the Gospels*, *Introducing New Testament Interpretation*, and *The Face of New Testament Studies*. McKnight's most recent books include the award-winning *The Jesus Creed* and *Embracing Grace*.

McKnight's flight back to Chicago wasn't scheduled for a few hours, so we took chairs facing each other and settled in for our conversation. I began by observing that there are some people who seem to uncritically accept the Bible without question. "Is that a good idea?" I asked.

"It's a good idea to trust the Bible, but we gain trust because we gain confidence to trust the Bible," he replied. "And sometimes that takes time. We ought to study the Bible carefully—and we should follow our questions."

My thoughts turned to *The Da Vinci Code*. "What about people who read Dan Brown's book and are willing to accept that without really questioning it?" I asked.

"It's an amazing phenomenon—the number of people who love *The Da Vinci Code*, and this is, I think, one of the most important questions we need to ask about this book. Why is everyone reading it and why do people want to believe it?

"I think the operative word here is 'suspicion.' Over the last century, many have become suspicious of the church and what the church has done. Think of the scandals involving Roman Catholic priests, scandals among televangelists, and the rise of the women's movement. I also think many people have been hurt by the church, and they see things in *The Da Vinci Code* that they want to hear. Add this to the post-modernity movement and its questioning of truth, as well as the rise of pluralism—all these things filter into why people want to read and believe what is in *The Da Vinci Code*. Even though it's not good history, people still want to believe its general message."

"So would you say people should read both *The Da Vinci Code* and the Bible critically?"

"Yes," he replied. "*The Da Vinci Code* has to be read as a piece of literature, as a page-turner, as a novel, as a great adventure, but at the same time, readers have to be suspicious. They have to read critically what Dan Brown has to say about history."

That seemed like a good entrée into issues involving the Gospels. "Well, he writes a lot about the New Testament," I commented. "You're a scholar in that area. To what degree do you believe these Gospels to be essentially reliable as history?"

McKnight's response was unambiguous and unequivocal. "I've been studying the Gospels as a matter of history for over thirty years, and I've come to the conviction that the four Gospels we have in the New Testament are essentially reliable accounts of the life and teachings of Jesus."

That kind of solid endorsement begged to be scrutinized. "There are others who would disagree with you," I pointed out. "Why should we believe you and not them?" With that, the conversation continued to unfold:

McKnight: Well, we can only measure these sorts of things by testing the evidence, by examining the kinds of things historians use to determine whether something is credible, trustworthy, and reliable. And I think it can be said that the canons [or criteria] of history that are used in all disciplines, if applied fairly to the Gospels, will show that the Gospels are reliable.

Q: *You're claiming that Matthew, Mark, Luke, and John are essentially reliable, but Dan Brown makes the claim that there were a lot more gospels than those four. In fact, he says there were over eighty gospels, and that Constantine got rid of the ones that said Jesus was just a mortal human being and only kept the ones that suited his agenda. That left Matthew, Mark, Luke, and John—the ones that emphasize Jesus' supernatural side and claim he's the Son of God. What about that? If we have a skewed deck from which to retrace history, then we can't really trust it, can we?*

McKnight: One of the alarming parts of Dan Brown's so-called historical treatment of the rise of the Bible and the Gospels is that he claims that there were eighty gospels, from which people voted on which ones were most reliable. No one knows where he came up with eighty, because there aren't that many. But what is most alarming is that the gospels that were not included in the New Testament are, in fact, much more supernatural. They present Jesus as much more magical than anything close to what we find in the New Testament.

So, in reality, his point is completely off base, because there is no evidence to support the idea that the gospels that were thrown away talk more about Jesus as a human being and the Gospels that we have talk more about Jesus as divine. It's quite the opposite, as a matter of fact. The Gospels that are included in our New Testament emphasize his humanity and his deity, whereas the gospels that didn't get included are so incredibly supernatural that he's no longer walking on planet Earth.

Q: So these other gospels—the Gospel of Thomas, the Gospel of Philip, the Gospel of Mary Magdalene, and so forth—in your view do not have the credibility that the four Gospels in the Bible have. But if they exist, shouldn't we be giving them equal weight with the gospels of Matthew, Mark, Luke, and John?

McKnight: What made a gospel reliable was that it was connected to the apostles; it was read by all the churches; and [it was] recognized as what Christians had always known about Jesus. Whereas the gospels that are not in the New Testament are elitist, esoteric, [and] talk about Jesus in ways that are not credible, and the theology of those books is not at all consistent with what the early Christian's faith was like.

Q: You're saying that Matthew, Mark, Luke, and John, because they have a connection with apostles—in other words, people who personally knew Jesus and the events they refer to—are more reliable?

McKnight: When Jesus said the things that he said, and when he did the things that he did, people walked away remembering and talking about what Jesus said and did. Those memories were passed on in a Jewish world, from person to person, and became the Gospels that we have. Here's the fact. Jesus spoke, Jesus acted. The early apostles remembered what Jesus said and did. The

Jewish world was fantastic at remembering these things. The Gospels are the result of a long process of early Christians getting together, telling one another what was going on, and this memory of the apostles became literary text—and they were all formed by 70 or 80 AD, within a generation of the life of Jesus. These are the Gospels that stuck and shaped the story of early Christianity. The second-, third-, and fourth-century gospels were attempts to make Jesus fit into another set of theological categories. The Gospels, however, gave rise to the orthodox Christian creeds that we all now confess.

Q: So if we're really looking for information about Jesus that we can trust, we would want to go back to these earliest documents that are rooted in the memories of the followers of Jesus—and these would be Matthew, Mark, Luke, and John?

McKnight: People knew what Jesus said, and if you started making things up about Jesus, there were eyewitnesses who would have said, "No, that's not what he said. No, that's not what he did. *This* is what he said and did. Everybody knows this."

Q: Well, did Dan Brown get it right that Constantine was the one who made the decisions about which gospels were included in the New Testament?

McKnight: This is embarrassing. This is a howler on the part of Dan Brown. Constantine had nothing whatsoever to do with the decision of which books are included in the New Testament. That decision was made far earlier than Constantine, even though it was a long process that wasn't actually finally determined until about fifty years after Constantine. But the four Gospels that we have today were in use from the first century. They are the only Gospels that all Christians used from the very beginning.

Q: *There was never a time when Matthew, Mark, Luke, and John were not considered reliable by the church?*

McKnight: That's exactly right. They were always the apostolic testimony to Jesus.

3. Read the *Da Vinci Code* quote below. How does the book portray the Bible? Do you believe the Bible was written by God, people, or a combination of the two? Explain.

> "The Bible is a product of *man*, my dear. Not of God....
> Man created it as a historical record of tumultuous times,
> and it has evolved through countless translations,
> additions, and revisions. History has never had
> a definitive version of the book."

Using Later Gospels

"The writings Brown uses to paint his picture of what Jesus was really like were written by adherents of Gnostic versions of Christianity. This thinking flourished during the second and third centuries, which means, then, that these writings ... come from the same period—more than *a hundred years after* Jesus' ministry, far later than any of the New Testament books.... Why in the world should we should believe that these *later* documents tell us more about events than *earlier* documents?... They are simply not useful for trying to understand Jesus' ministry and the shape of very early Christianity."

Historian Amy Welborn in *De-Coding Da Vinci*

Key Word: Gnosticism

"Gnosticism [was] an early Greek religious movement that was particularly influential in the second-century church. The word *Gnosticism* comes from the Greek term *gnosis*, meaning 'knowledge.' Gnostics believed that devotees had gained a special kind of spiritual enlightenment, through which they had attained a secret or higher level of knowledge not accessible to the uninitiated.... Gnostic documents [such as those used by Brown] represent neither the earliest nor most authentic materials about Jesus and his followers.... [They] were written late in the second century or even in the third century AD."

New Testament scholar Ben Witherington III in *The Gospel Code*

The Gnostic Gospels

"Some of (Dan Brown's) most important texts are the various Gnostic gospels, which he uncritically accepts as accurate accounts of Jesus' life.... They were late arrivals, which is one reason why church leaders rejected them.... They lacked authority since their authors were neither (a) apostles of Jesus nor (b) persons associated with apostles of Jesus.... No one really knows who wrote the texts."

Richard Abanes in *The Truth Behind the Da Vinci Code*

Chapter 2

4. Why do you think it was important to establish the canon, or the official list of books in the Bible? What criteria would you have used to determine which gospels should be included?

Putting Together the New Testament

Consider the following brief sketch of how the New Testament canon came to be:

1. Letters from apostles were written and received in the churches; copies were made and circulated.
2. A growing group of books developed that were recognized as inspired Scripture. Important questions for their acceptance included: Was the book written by either an apostle or someone who knew the apostles and thus had the stamp of apostolic authority? Was it in harmony with other accepted doctrine?
3. By the end of the first century, all 27 books in our present canon had been written and received by the churches. Though some of the canonical lists were incomplete, this is not always to be interpreted as the rejection of some books. Often it simply means that some books were unknown in certain areas.
4. A generation after the end of the apostolic age, every book of the New Testament had been cited as authoritative by some church father.
5. Remaining doubts or debates over certain books continued into the fourth century. The first time the list of our 27 books

5. How significant is it that the four Gospels in the New Testament have roots in the eyewitness accounts of people who knew Jesus and saw his miracles and post-resurrection appearances?

The Dead Sea Scrolls

"Some of the gospels that Constantine attempted to eradicate managed to survive. The Dead Sea Scrolls were found in the 1950s.... The Vatican, in keeping with their tradition of misinformation, tried very hard to suppress the release of these scrolls."

The Da Vinci Code

"Constantine was not in the business of eradicating any gospels. The Dead Sea Scrolls were discovered in 1947, not the 1950s. And they did not contain any gospels or any references to Jesus."

Historian Paul Maier
in *The Da Vinci Code: Fact or Fiction?*

The Evidence for Reliability

Hank Hanegraaff of the Christian Research Institute makes a strong case for the Bible's reliability, using three areas of evidence:

- **Manuscript Evidence**. The New Testament documents have stronger manuscript support than any other work of classical literature, including works of Homer, Plato, Aristotle, Caesar, and Tacitus. Furthermore, the reliability of the Gospel accounts is confirmed through the eyewitness credentials of the authors. Finally, secular historians — including Josephus (before AD 100), the Roman Tacitus (c. AD 120), the Roman Suetonius (c. AD 110), and the Roman governor Pliny the Younger (c. AD 110) — confirm many of the events, people, places, and customs chronicled in the New Testament.
- **Archaeological Evidence**. Archaeology is a powerful witness to the accuracy of biblical documents, confirming scores of references.
- **Evidence from Messianic Prophecies**. The Bible records predictions of events that could not have been known or predicted by chance or common sense.

6. To what extent do you consider the Bible to be reliable and God's authoritative Word? To what extent do you consider *The Da Vinci Code* to be reliable? In each case, what is the basis for your level of trust or distrust?

Dr. McKnight's interview was helpful in dispelling some of the misinformation in *The Da Vinci Code*, but there were still questions on my mind. I wanted to delve deeper into the issue of historical bias, for example, and ask what McKnight would suggest to someone who's really interested in getting at the truth about the Gospels. Since the genial McKnight seemed to be enjoying our discussion, I moved ahead.

"You claimed earlier that Matthew, Mark, Luke, and John are more reliable than the Gnostic gospels Brown cites because they're rooted in eyewitness testimony and they're dated much closer to the events. But aren't they somewhat biased?" I asked. "If they're written by people who were already followers of Jesus, how can we really trust that they're not too biased to be reliable?"

"The gospels *are* biased," McKnight bluntly answered. "Because all narrative about Jesus takes the data and the facts and puts them into a narrative in order to interpret them and give meaning to those events. This is the story of Jesus. Is there any other way to tell the story of someone who was a miracle-working, marginalized-including, and reconciling person, who gave himself away and was raised from the dead? Is there anything other than to tell the story of a Messiah and a Lord and a Son of God? Yes, that's the bias, because that's where the facts fell out. That's what history is.

"From the very beginning, when people heard Jesus and watched him, they tried to make sense of him. And the only categories that made sense were: 'This has got to be the Messiah. This has got to be the Lord. This has got to be the Son of God.' They couldn't very well say, 'Well, this is just a teacher. This [man] is just like Plato, or just like Aristotle.' They had to have other categories to explain their cognitive schema. What kind of person is this? Who is Jesus?"

I had to ask a clarifying question. "And the end result, you believe, is a set of four Gospels that are essentially trustworthy?"

"Yes, a trustworthy, reliable understanding of who Jesus was," he replied. "But they are clearly a presentation of Jesus as the Son of God."

Brown vs. History

Yet that's not Brown's view. "Dan Brown paints a picture of history that is totally at odds with what the Gospels in the Bible claim actually took place," I pointed out. "Why not believe Brown's version?"

"One thing Dan Brown will admit is that the Gospels' presentation of Jesus is consistent with what Christians have always believed about Jesus," McKnight replied. "But that is not, for him, the only picture of Jesus. The only way he can get another picture of Jesus is to add to the Gospels in the Bible with gospels that are not considered authentic and are not reliable history—or to subtract from the Gospels that we have. And one of the underlying themes of *The Da Vinci Code* is that the Gospel records distorted the facts of history—distorted facts about Mary Magdalene, distorted facts about Jesus. But any time we test the Gospel records themselves with modern historical criteria, they come up smelling pretty good."

"What would some of the criteria be to determine whether or not these Gospels are reliable?" I asked.

"Whether they fit a first-century Jewish context," he said. "Whether they're the sort of thing that is consistent from one end to the other of the Gospels. Whether there are multiple witnesses to the same event. For instance, Matthew, Mark, Luke, and John each testify to the resurrection with independent stories. These sorts of criteria are what historians have always used to measure whether a text is recording reliable history or not."

If the Gospels truly can be trusted, though, that leaves another issue. "If God is really behind the Bible," I said, "then why do so many people still have confusion and doubts about it?"

"I don't think enough people ask the question honestly about the resurrection of Jesus and the credibility of eyewitnesses who were there and who would vouch for the character of Jesus and the character of the early Christians.

"But, without doubt, in order to believe the Gospels and their portrait about Jesus requires faith. As St. Augustine said, 'We believe in order to understand.' And over my years of teaching the Bible, I've become convinced that the problem with believing the Bible is not based on what we *don't* understand about the Bible—but it's based on what we *do* understand about the Bible.

"What we do understand challenges everything about us. Jesus calls us to follow him, and that means we have to give up our life. That, I think, is the major reason why people don't want to believe in the Gospels, because it involves self-surrender, the hardest thing in life to do. It involves loving God, loving others, and surrendering our lives to what God has called us to do."

"And," I said, "that's very challenging."

"*Extremely* challenging," McKnight stressed.

"Still," I said, "if someone were to embark on an investigation of the Bible, and really wanted to get at the truth behind these issues, what suggestions would you give for how to proceed?"

"First," he said, "I would ask him to read the Gospels and trust the Gospels and see where that takes him."

In a way, I was taken aback by a scholar—who has spent a lifetime studying the historical credentials of the Gospels—offering such an experiential approach. I tried to summarize his point to make sure I understood it.

"In a sense," I said, "you're not only saying there are good historical reasons to believe that the Gospels are reliable, but in addition, we should really experience what the Gospels are talking about—as the Old Testament says, 'Taste and see that the Lord is good.' We test them by putting enough trust in them to live out this faith experiment and see where it takes us."

"That's what I believe," he said. "I believe that people listened to Jesus, they trusted him, and they found that what he had to say was true. I believe in the Gospels not only because after thirty years of studying them I find them to be reliable over and over again—but because in studying the Gospels, I encountered Jesus.

"And the Jesus who I've encountered has changed my life."

7. Some people argue that because the Gospels in the Bible can be traced back to followers of Jesus, the books are biased and contain distorted historical information that agrees with the followers' preconceived notions. Do you agree with this reasoning? Why or why not?

8. If God is really behind the Bible, why do you think he hasn't eliminated any doubts or confusion about that?

9. Many people testify to the life-changing message they encounter in the Bible. What are the strengths and weaknesses of using that as a basis for validating the trustworthiness of the Bible? Address the same question regarding *The Da Vinci Code*.

Bible Challenges

"A thousand times over, the death knell of the Bible has been sounded, the funeral procession formed, the inscription cut on the tombstone, and the committal read. But somehow the corpse never stays put."

Theologian Bernard Ramm

10. What would motivate you to embark on an investigation to determine once and for all the truth behind *The Da Vinci Code* and the Bible? Where would you begin?

11. What would it take for you to place complete confidence in the Bible as truth from God and as the authoritative guide for your life? What difference would it make in your everyday life to believe that the Bible is God's Word?

McKnight and I continued to chat until it was time for him to leave for the airport. After seeing him off, I climbed into my car and headed home on the freeway—which gave me plenty of idle time in California rush-hour traffic to reflect on our conversation.

When I investigated the reliability of the New Testament as an inquisitive atheist, I came to the same conclusion as McKnight: the Gospels can be trusted when they report on Jesus, including his miracles and resurrection from the dead. While my book *The Case for Christ* goes into far more detail, there were basically four categories of evidence that inexorably led me to that conclusion:

- There's persuasive evidence that the Gospels are rooted in direct and indirect eyewitness testimony. There are strong reasons to conclude that the material in the gospels of Matthew and John can be traced back to the disciples whose names they bear; that the gospel of Mark reflects the testimony of the disciple Peter as reported by his close associate John Mark; and that Luke, sort of a first-century investigative reporter, gathered information for his gospel from those around Jesus and also from his close companion Paul, who himself had encountered the resurrected Christ.

- The Gospels were written so close to the events—in fact, I believe earlier than McKnight's estimate—that they can't be merely legendary. What's more, most of Paul's writings come earlier than the Gospels, and they incorporate even earlier Christian creeds and hymns that affirm Jesus' resurrection and deity.

- The Gospels contain embarrassing material about the disciples and hard-to-explain sayings by Jesus that certainly would have been edited out if the writers felt the freedom to manipulate or whitewash the record. Yet they're included—why? Because that's what happened, and the writers were committed to reporting the truth even when it was uncomfortable.

- Archaeology and ancient writings outside the Bible tend to corroborate the accuracy of the Gospels. In his book *The Historical Jesus*, Gary Habermas cites a total of thirty-nine ancient sources documenting the life of Jesus, from which he enumerates more than one hundred reported facts concerning Jesus' life, teachings, crucifixion, and resurrection.

None of the later and fanciful Gnostic gospels, which Brown credulously touts in *The Da Vinci Code*, come anywhere close to matching the credentials of the four biblical Gospels. They were written at least 150 to 200 years after the events they purport to describe and thus have no ties to eyewitnesses; bear the obvious earmarks of legendary development; and are hopelessly tainted by esoteric theological agendas. In fact, it's really a misnomer to even call them "gospels." No wonder the uniform testimony of the early church was that the four Gospels of the New Testament contain the very best data about Jesus.

Even the critical German scholar Peter Stuhlmacher said recently: "We have good reasons to treat the Gospels seriously as a source of information on the life and teachings of Jesus, and thus on the historical origins of Christianity."

I'd encourage anyone, including you, to investigate the credentials of the four Gospels with an open mind—and then ask yourself this life-changing question: "What is the central message that these ancient writings have for me personally?"

Chapter 3

WHAT'S THE ROLE OF WOMEN IN CHRISTIANITY?

You do ill if you praise, but worse if you censure,
what you do not understand.
Leonardo da Vinci

Between Fleet Street and the River Thames in London, amid modern office buildings and crowds of briefcase-toting pedestrians, Garry and I came upon an unlikely oasis: an imposing, tan-colored, 800-year-old church, much of it round like a castle's tower—a site we quickly recognized as the scene of a heart-pounding encounter in *The Da Vinci Code* as opposing forces pursued the Holy Grail.

Many of Dan Brown's facts about the Temple Church are accurate. For instance, there's no dispute that it was built by the Knights Templar, the Crusaders who protected holy places in Palestine, provided security for pilgrims going to the Holy Land, and became wealthy bankers. Garry and I quickly found evidence of their legacy as we gained entry to the church and closely examined its interior.

For instance, the round structure of the church's oldest section, which was consecrated in 1185 by the patriarch of Jerusalem, was intended to reflect the circular design of the place considered most holy by the Crusaders: Jerusalem's Church of the Holy Sepulcher.

Then there are the nine chilling stone effigies of ancient knights embedded in the floor of the church. Several are anonymous, but Garry bent down to study the inscription on one impressive knight who was depicted preparing to draw his sword.

"Lee—take a look at this!" he called over to me.

I knelt and looked at the brass plate: sure enough, it was William the Marshal, Earl of Pembroke, the soldier and statesman who has been called the greatest knight who ever lived. He fought five hundred bloody tournament bouts during his life, but was never defeated. He also negotiated between King John and the barons, which led to John's signing of the Magna Carta. When William died in 1219, he insisted on being buried in Temple Church as a Knights Templar. The 2001 film *A Knight's Tale* featured several events from his life.

Yet numerous assertions by Brown about the Knights Templar are vigorously disputed by historians. For example, they challenge his claims that the Knights Templar was formed by the Priory of Sion (which we discovered in the first chapter didn't even exist until 1956) and was focused on protecting the secrets about Mary Magdalene's marriage to Jesus and the fact that he wanted her to lead his church.

At the heart of Brown's novel and movie are the allegations that power-hungry men stole the church from Mary Magdalene; intentionally and maliciously destroyed her reputation by falsely branding her a whore; and systematically obliterated the "sacred feminine" core of Christianity, ultimately leading to the church devaluing and squelching women through the centuries.

Jesus, according to Brown, was the "original feminist" who was thwarted in trying to create a matriarchal church. In reality, contends Brown, the Holy Grail isn't the cup used by Jesus at the Last Supper, but actually refers to "the quest to kneel before the bones of Magdalene," who bore Jesus' bloodline.

All of this raises important issues. For example, is there any historical evidence that suggests Mary Magdalene was the wife of Jesus and that together they had a daughter named Sarah? If not, who was Mary—really? What was Jesus' true attitude toward women—and has the church lived up to the ideals he embodied? Was the "sacred feminine" an essential part of earliest Christianity?

These questions led me to a scholar whose book, *Women as Christ's Disciples*, explores the unique contribution that women—including Mary Magdalene—made to the ministry of Jesus.

1. Compare and contrast the book, *The Da Vinci Code*, with the movie based on it. Which did you like better? Why?

Constantine's Mission?

"Powerful men in the early Christian church 'conned' the world by propagating lies that devalued the female.... Constantine and his male successors successfully converted the world from matriarchal paganism to patriarchal Christianity by waging a campaign of propaganda that demonized the sacred feminine."

The Da Vinci Code

Jesus' Mission?

"Nowhere in serious scholarly work do we find anyone taking seriously the suggestion that Jesus' mission was all about sending forth Mary Magdalene to carry his message of the 'sacred feminine.'"

Historian Amy Welborn in *De-Coding Da Vinci*

2. Throughout *The Da Vinci Code*, a concept called the "sacred feminine" is referenced. Describe what you think the "sacred feminine" is all about. Do you have a positive, negative, or neutral viewpoint toward the idea? Explain.

The soft-spoken and thoughtful Dr. Katherine McReynolds, a professional dancer before entering academia, received her master's degree in theology from the Talbot School of Theology and then went on to earn her doctorate in religion and social ethics at the University of Southern California. In her fascinating dissertation, which became a book published by University Press of America, she explores concepts of the soul, drawing upon the theories of Aristotle, Francis Bacon, and others, and examines whether biotechnology can ever bring happiness through genetic enhancements.

She has been a faculty member at the Torrey Honors Institute at Biola University in La Mirada, California, and currently serves as an adjunct professor at Biola.

However, I sought her for an interview because of her expertise in dealing with issues involving women. Her books include biographies of influential Christian women Catherine Marshall and Susanna Wesley, and she is a contributor on the Gospels to the Women's Evangelical Library. What particularly caught my attention was her book *Women as Christ's Disciples*, coauthored with A. Boyd Luter, in which she analyzes historical information about Mary Magdalene and other women followers of Jesus.

The setting for our interview was a bit unusual—a house owned by a Southern California university to provide a place for students and professors of philosophy to gather and discuss Kierkegaard, Plato, and other great thinkers. On this day, though, I wasn't looking for heady theories—I was after concrete historical data that could shed light on Jesus and his relationship with women.

Jesus, the Feminist?

I started with a fundamental point made in *The Da Vinci Code*. "Dr. McReynolds," I asked, "isn't Dan Brown partially right when he says that Jesus was the original feminist?"

"I wouldn't go so far as to say Jesus was the original feminist," came her response, "but he certainly was revolutionary in his views toward women, especially given the time and place in which he lived. He treated women with a certain dignity and raised them to a level of respect in society that was really unheard of in his day. Women were included in his public ministry and they were invited to minister to his needs and the needs of his disciples; they gave him financial support and engaged him in public discourse. So Jesus was definitely revolutionary in his treatment of women.

"Now, the church has done a pretty good job, over-all, in acknowledging and encouraging the contributions of women, although without any doubt there have been stretches of time where they might not have been acknowledged to the extent that they should. But it wouldn't be fair to call it suppression. That would not be a fair assessment."

An interesting analysis, I thought to myself, coming from a woman scholar. I opened *The Da Vinci Code* and found the place I had previously marked. "Here's a quote from Dan Brown's novel, where he talks about women and Genesis," I said, and then I read the words of character Robert Langdon:

> "The power of the female and her ability to produce life was once very sacred, but it posed a threat to the rise of the predominantly male Church, and so the sacred feminine was demonized and called unclean. It was *man*, not God, who created the concept of 'original sin,' whereby Eve tasted of the apple and caused the downfall of the human race. Woman, once the sacred giver of life, was now the enemy."

I closed the book. "Is that what happened?" I asked McReynolds.

"That is a completely misguided view of the way it happened," she said.

I pressed her: "What about this idea that the church views women as the enemy?"

"The church in no way views women as the enemy. That's ridiculous," she insisted. "The enemy was very clearly the serpent in the garden. If you want to call anybody or anything the enemy, it would have to be the serpent, not women. Certainly women have not been viewed as an enemy in the church."

"Dan Brown talks a lot about the sacred feminine," I said. "To what degree was this present among the early Christians?"

She was blunt. "It wasn't present at all."

"It wasn't at all?" I asked.

"Not at all, period," she confirmed. "From the first century into the second-century Gnostic writings, through the third century, it is simply not there. In fact, there is evidence quite the contrary, that from the first century on, Jesus and his followers referred to God as Father."

I wanted to be crystal clear. "So if we go back to Jesus, this idea of the sacred feminine is not found in his teachings, or in his life in his first-century ministry, or what we see reflected in the Gospels?"

"Not in the teachings of Jesus, not in the writings of Paul, not even in the writings from the Gnostic gospels of the second and third centuries. It's simply not there."

"It seems ironic," I continued, "that Dan Brown likes to quote a lot from these later and historically unreliable gospels, yet these very gospels are the ones in which women are viewed less favorably than we see Jesus treating them in the biblical Gospels."

"That's exactly right," she said. "That's what you're going to find if you take the time to really read them. From the Gospel of Thomas to the Gospel of Mary, women are not viewed in a very favorable light at all."

With this background settled, it was time to move on to the *Da Vinci Code* topic that gets the most press: Jesus and his relationship with Mary Magdalene.

Was Jesus Married?

I began by asking: "Dan Brown says that the marriage of Jesus and Mary Magdalene is part of the historical record, and that the biggest cover-up in human history is that he fathered a child through her. Do you believe there is credible historical evidence that Jesus and Mary Magdalene really were married?"

Again, McReynolds was direct. "There is," she said, "not a shred of credible evidence at all."

"Nothing?"

"Not a thing. Not in the four Gospels, not in Paul's writings. And Paul even writes about marriage. If Jesus were married, you would certainly think that Paul would at least mention it since he addresses marriage in the book of 1 Corinthians."

I knew that in 1 Corinthians 9:5, Paul was defending the right to have a wife: "Do we not have the right to be accompanied by a wife, as the other apostles, and the brothers of the Lord and Cephas [Peter]?" The clear implication is if Jesus had been married, Paul would have undoubtedly cited him as the prime example: "If the Master was married, then we can be too." But his silence speaks volumes.

McReynolds continued. "You don't see Jesus being married in any of the second- or third-century Gnostic gospels either. It is not mentioned anywhere."

That last point was particularly interesting in light of Brown's strong reliance on these apocryphal Gnostic gospels. "So," I said, "even in the gospels that aren't included in the Bible—the ones that don't have the same historical credibility that the Gospels in the Bible have—we still don't see the marriage of Jesus, is that correct?"

"There's not a single mention," she affirmed. "And you would think that such an important issue would be mentioned. But there is not a single shred of evidence that he was married."

What If . . .

I decided to ask the "what if" question: What if Jesus and Mary Magdalene *had* been married—would this create any theological problems?

I was aware of Christian scholars who wouldn't see any difficulty if Jesus had been married, even though they see no evidence that he actually was wed to anyone. When I asked historian Paul Maier for his opinion during the interview I conducted for the first chapter of this book, this was his response:

I don't think there is anything wrong with the concept of Jesus being married. Marriage, after all, was invented by God. The problem is this: One of the functions of marriage is to produce children, and that leads to a theological problem. Can't you see Jesus talking to his oldest son, saying, "Well, Samuel, you are only one-quarter God and three-quarters man, and your son, Jacob, in turn, is only going to be one-eighth God." We'd have a terrible theological problem. So I think it's much better that Jesus didn't get married. And he did not.

When I pursued the issue with McReynolds, she said she *did* believe it would make a theological difference if Jesus had been married.

"It is not that there is anything wrong or sinful with the idea of marriage," she explained. "The point is that Jesus had a special mission—a very unique mission—as the Son of God and the Savior of the world, and he stands in a long tradition of prophets that were set aside by special vows to God. And so I think it does make a theological difference that he remained single and totally devoted to his mission."

I wanted to make sure I understood her completely. "So, you're saying that he was in a line of tradition where people would consecrate themselves to God or have a vow of chastity so that their lives would be focused only on God and his mission for them here on earth?"

"Absolutely," she replied. "He definitely stands in that tradition, much like John the Baptist."

I asked, "What about Dan Brown's assertion that a rabbi in the first century would never be single and, therefore, Jesus must have been married?"

"Well, that doesn't hold much weight because in the community of the saints in the first century, you had many rabbis and Jewish teachers who were not married. It was not required that they marry. In fact, there is quite a bit of evidence that there were many rabbis who weren't married."

"What about Dan Brown's contention that *The Last Supper* painting by Leonardo Da Vinci 'practically shouts at the viewer that Jesus and Mary Magdalene were a pair?'" I asked. "Does the painting shout that to you?"

"No, it doesn't. And it doesn't shout it to most art historians either. Many art historians recognize this as John the apostle for three reasons. First, John is not seen anywhere else in the painting. Secondly, John is often depicted as being more feminine looking. And third, and probably most importantly, Leonardo Da Vinci himself recognized this as John the apostle, and he said so in his early sketches."

That last point seemed to sink a dagger through the heart of Brown's claim. "So, his early sketches actually indicated that this was John, not Mary Magdalene?"

"Yes, that is correct," she said.

"Well," I commented, "that's pretty authoritative, I would say."

"I would say so," she concluded. "Directly from the artist himself."

3. *The Da Vinci Code* charges that over the past two thousand years, Christianity has been virulently anti-woman and determined to stamp out any hints of the "sacred feminine." To what extent do you agree or disagree with this allegation and why?

4. What was your initial reaction when you first heard the claim that Jesus had been married to Mary Magdalene? Do you think they were really married? Do you believe such a union—if it had actually occurred—would have created any theological problems? Why or why not?

5. To what extent do you think Eve caused humanity's downfall? Do you think the Bible holds Eve, or the whole human race, responsible for sin? Explain. In what ways, if any, does the church view women as the enemy?

An Eternal Debt?

"It seemed Eve's bite from the apple of knowledge was a debt women were doomed to pay for eternity."
The Da Vinci Code

Humanity's Downfall?

"Christianity does not declare that Eve caused humanity's downfall. The church teaches that the Fall came through Eve and Adam—particularly Adam because he deliberately chose to disobey God."

Robert Abanes in
The Truth Behind the Da Vinci Code

6. To what extent have women been treated like second-class citizens in the past? How are women treated unfairly in our world today? Are there ways in which you believe women are still treated unfairly within Christianity?

7. *The Da Vinci Code* asserts that Mary Magdalene was "shunned" and "demonized" by the church. Do you agree with this charge? Why or why not?

Breaking the Mold

"I agree that historically the church can be faulted for not giving women their rightful place in Christian ministry.... Jesus did reject those cultural taboos that put women in a disrespected place as second-class citizens of the Kingdom. Women in Scripture are equal with men, though their roles are different.... Jesus broke the mold, elevating women to a place of respect and honor."

Erwin Lutzer in *The Da Vinci Deception*

8. *The Da Vinci Code* says, "*The Last Supper* practically shouts at the viewer that Jesus and Magdalene were a pair." Do agree with this assessment of Da Vinci's painting?

As I continued my interview with Dr. McReynolds, again I picked up my copy of *The Da Vinci Code* and quoted from its dialogue, with the character Sir Leigh Teabing initially speaking:

"At this point in the gospels, Jesus suspects He will soon be captured and crucified. So He gives Mary Magdalene instructions on how to carry on His Church after He is gone. As a result, Peter expresses his discontent over playing second fiddle to a woman. I daresay Peter was something of a sexist...."

Sophie looked at him. "You're saying the Christian Church was to be carried on by a *woman*?"

"That was the plan.... He intended for the future of
His Church to be in the hands of Mary Magdalene."

I looked up at McReynolds. "Is there any evidence historically that this was Jesus' intent?" I asked.

"No. [According to Brown] this idea of Mary being
given the power of the church comes from the Gospel
of Mary Magdalene, which is a Gnostic gospel written in
the latter part of the second century. In that gospel, Mary
is given a vision—a revelation by Jesus—and it does not
have to do with her being given the mission to lead the
church. It has to do with finding salvation for souls."

"So you're saying that *inside* the Bible and *outside* the
Bible, there is not one bit of evidence in history for this
assertion that Jesus wanted Mary Magdalene to run the
church."

Again, she stood firm. "No, there is not. There definitely is not."

Yet many Christians believe to this day that Mary
Magdalene had been a prostitute before meeting Jesus,
which Brown claims is the product of a campaign by the
church to demonize, shun, and discredit her. When I
asked McReynolds about this, she replied:

"This idea [that Mary had been a prostitute] comes
from a sermon that was given by Pope Gregory the Great
five hundred years after the Gospels were written. In
that sermon, he refers to the prostitute who is found in
Luke 7 as being Mary Magdalene. However, most scholars agree that this cannot be her for one primary reason:
Luke doesn't even introduce Mary Magdalene for the

first time until chapter 8. So the prostitute Pope Gregory talked about could not be Mary Magdalene.

"Regardless," she continued, "I don't think Pope Gregory's purpose in talking about Mary Magdalene and referring to her as a prostitute was to demonize her in any way. I think he was setting her up to illustrate that if Jesus could forgive a prostitute, then he could forgive the average sinner as well."

"So Mary wasn't a prostitute after all."

"There's no evidence she was a prostitute. The only thing we know about her background, essentially, was that she had seven demons that Jesus cast out of her. This is referenced in Luke 8."

"How should Mary Magdalene be viewed today?" I asked.

"She was the first and the most prominent witness of his resurrection, and she goes back to the disciples to tell them about it. She was loyal. She leaves a legacy. And what is more interesting, too, is that in John 10, Jesus is portrayed as the Great Shepherd and says his disciples hear his voice. When Mary is at his tomb and Jesus speaks her name, she recognizes him. This indicates that she is not only a witness, but a follower and a learner of Christ. And then she goes on to proclaim it.

"So on one hand she is taking on and assuming roles which were revolutionary in that time—to sit at the feet of a first-century Jewish rabbi. But she also maintains her traditional roles, in terms of hospitality and serving food. But those roles are given new significance, as she was serving those in the kingdom of God."

The Gap and the Trend

My final line of questions to McReynolds was prompted by my conversations with some women who have read *The Da Vinci Code* and have found themselves resonating with its strong feminist themes.

"Let's say there's a woman who reads *The Da Vinci Code* and puts down the book and says, 'I knew it! The church is anti-woman. The church is opposed to women having any positions of influence whatsoever in society. This just confirms my worst suspicions about Christians.' As a woman and as a Christian, how would you respond to that?"

"I can see how Dan Brown would evoke those kinds of responses in women. There is no question about it," she admitted.

"But, in reality, nothing could be further from the truth. As a wife of eighteen years with three kids, as an active participant in my church, and as a professor and a scholar, I have the freedom to be who I am as a woman and a follower of Jesus.

"I am not considered in any way—whether in the church or in my job or in the home—as a second-class citizen. I am considered equal with men in those arenas —and I have to say, in my experience in the church and the ministry, equal in the eyes of God. My role may be different, but that's okay. And I think there is an element of freedom within Christianity that Dan Brown is missing. He's really missing the whole point."

"Wouldn't you concede, though, that there is a gap between the attitude that Jesus displayed toward women and the way the church has fallen short in living up to that ideal?"

"Oh, I agree there is a gap," she said, "but that gap is closing, and it has been closing over the past several decades. Women have many more opportunities today than they have had in previous centuries."

"And you see this trend continuing?" I asked.

"I do. I see women stepping out more and more and being involved in ministry in areas that they haven't done in decades past — and that's a good thing."

That was encouraging, coming as it was from a scholar who's also a woman. In fact, her response prompted me to cap our conversation with one last question: "After reading Dan Brown's book, one can't help but feel a sense of pessimism about the church. Yet you sound very optimistic."

"I *am* optimistic, because I'm confident in the reality of how much respect the church has for women and our contribution to the kingdom," she replied.

"Dan Brown is a fiction writer — and he writes good fiction. But when it comes to the reality of how women are viewed and the history of the church's treatment of women, he's missed the mark."

9. If you were grading the church as a whole on how it has lived up to Jesus' attitudes toward women, what grade would you give and why?

10. If you had the power to make sweeping changes worldwide, what changes, if any, would you propose about the treatment of women both inside and outside the church? Explain.

Expected to Marry?

"Jesus was a Jew and the social decorum during that time virtually forbid a Jewish man to be unmarried.... If Jesus were not married, at least one of the Bible's gospels would have mentioned it."

The Da Vinci Code

"Marriage was certainly the rule and expectation for Jews. By the first century, there were exceptions to the rule.... It has long been believed by Christians and scholars that Jesus was single, and there are good reasons for this belief. When he was in ministry, there was no mention of a wife.... Jesus' family members—his mother, brothers, and sisters—were mentioned more than once, but never a wife. Nor was there any indication that he was widowed.... What was the likelihood that Jesus was married? The answer here is short—none."

Darrell Bock in *Breaking the Da Vinci Code*

What about Witch Hunts?

"The Catholic Inquisition published the . . . *Malleus Maleficarum* . . . (which) indoctrinated the world to 'the dangers of freethinking women' and instructed the clergy how to locate, torture, and destroy them. . . . During three hundred years of witch hunts, the Church burned at the stake an astounding five *million* women."

The Da Vinci Code

"This medieval book . . . was used to persecute both women *and men*. In fact, historical documents show that most of the victims 'were not killed by Catholics or officials of the Church,' but were executed by the state. Scholarly estimates put the number of 'witch hunt' victims in Europe . . . at 30,000 to 80,000. . . . Moreover 20 to 25 percent of those were male."

Richard Abanes in
The Truth Behind the Da Vinci Code

Few things are as depressing as being in romantic Paris without your spouse. But that's how I found myself on my journey to England and France to check out the locations that are featured in Dan Brown's novel and film. Still, it's hard not to act like a tourist in such a historic city, and so Garry and I made the obligatory visit to the Eiffel Tower and also found ourselves at the beautiful Notre Dame Cathedral.

That's when Garry made a powerful point. "*The Da Vinci Code* claims the church has devalued and dishonored women," he said as he pointed toward the church. "But Notre Dame means 'Our Lady'—it's a reference to

Mary, the mother of Jesus. How could Dan Brown possibly claim the church has failed to honor its significant women when throughout history the church has consistently held Mary in the highest esteem—even naming cathedrals and churches in her honor?"

That's a legitimate critique. And it's just one of many inconsistencies and inaccuracies regarding Brown's allegations about women and the church—and about Jesus supposedly having been married.

For instance, he relies on two late Gnostic "gospels" that lack any historical credibility—the Gospel of Philip (written two hundred years after Jesus' ministry) and the Gospel of Mary Magdalene (created at the end of the second century at the earliest)—and yet neither one of them actually says Jesus was ever wed to anyone. Besides, since these writings are steeped in Gnosticism, which saw sexual activity as inherently evil, they would have been repulsed by the very idea of such a union.

Brown says the word "companion" that's used to describe Jesus' relationship with Mary in the Gospel of Philip really means "spouse" in Aramaic. The problem is that this gospel wasn't written in Aramaic, as Brown claims—it was written in Coptic. Scholar Ben Witherington III says this particular word is borrowed from the Greek and most likely means "sister" in the spiritual sense.

As for Jesus supposedly kissing Mary Magdalene on the mouth, that's missing from the actual manuscript of the Gospel of Philip.

Also in the Gospel of Philip, the disciples say to Jesus about Mary Magdalene, "Why do you love her more than all of us?" Brown believes this suggests Jesus and Mary were husband and wife—but if they were, then the question would have been absurd to ask in the first place. If Jesus really were married, he would have replied: "Duh! She's my wife! Of course that's why I love her so much."

Brown's flimsy case for the marriage of Jesus simply dissolves under close inspection. However, there is a small seed of truth in what Brown said about Jesus: he really was a revolutionary in his attitudes toward women in a day when they were considered to have less than equal value. Says Rebecca Jones in her book *Does Christianity Squash Women?*:

> Jesus never slanders or belittles women. He does not make generalizations about them. He does not shut them out of conversations or ignore them. He doesn't make them feel small or relegate them to an inferior status. Everything he says and does in relation to women shows the utmost care and respect.

Has the church always lived up to those ideals? Unfortunately, no, and it should repent when mistakes are made. But the church's failures are a reflection on the human beings who run the institution, not on Jesus or his teachings.

As for me, I believe that both women *and* men can equally find hope in the real model of Christianity that's reflected in Galatians 3:28: "There is neither Jew nor Greek, slave nor free, male nor female, for you are all one in Christ Jesus."

Chapter 4

IS JESUS THE SON OF GOD?

The noblest pleasure is the joy of understanding.
Leonardo da Vinci

All through our investigation of the sites from *The Da Vinci Code* book and movie, we saw the symbolism again and again. From the baptismal font at the Lincoln Cathedral, carved out of solid marble in Belgium in the twelfth century, to the mosaics, gilded altars, and seven-foot figures of Christ and his apostles in the stained glass of Westminster Abbey—over and over, we encountered signs of Jesus being honored as the Son of God.

Belief in his divinity—which inspired many of the artists whose works hang in the Louvre and the authors who penned the worship songs in the hymnals at the Temple Church—is foundational to Christianity. Still, it's an *astonishing* claim. Is it the mere product of blind faith and wishful thinking—or is there historical evidence to back up that belief?

Here's where *The Da Vinci Code* makes its most startling charge: that Jesus' followers only considered him to be a human being until Emperor Constantine "upgraded" his status to deity almost three hundred years after his death. It's an astounding allegation—but is it historical revisionism or are there persuasive reasons to believe it's true?

Actually, Dan Brown's character, Sir Leigh Teabing, has many positive things to say about Jesus. He calls him "a historical figure of staggering influence, perhaps the most enigmatic and inspirational leader the world has ever seen." He was, said Teabing, "the prophesied Messiah" who "possessed a rightful claim to the throne of the King of the Jews."

Indeed, virtually every religion has nice things to say about Jesus. Muslims and Bahais consider him to be a great prophet. Hindus, Buddhists, and even some atheists find many of his teachings respectable. But Christians go further. His deity is not only at the core of their faith, but so is the belief that each person's eternal destiny hinges on his or her personal response to Jesus as God.

To examine Brown's claim about Constantine, and whether Jesus ever really made any claims of divinity about himself, I sat down with New Testament scholar Dr. Mark Strauss, who has both impressive credentials as well as an uncanny ability to communicate without academic jargon.

1. Who do you think Jesus was: a myth, a mere man, a great man, a wise teacher, a prophet, or God who became a man? What leads you to that conclusion?

2. *The Da Vinci Code* claims that Jesus' followers considered him to be "a great and powerful man, but a *man* nonetheless" and that it wasn't until the fourth century that he was deified. If this is true, what are the implications for Christianity?

The Human Side of Jesus

The Da Vinci Code alleges that Emperor Constantine omitted gospels that portrayed the human side of Jesus. However, here are descriptions found in the four Gospels of the Bible that affirm Jesus' human traits:

- He began life as a baby, born from a woman (Luke 2:6–7).
- He went through the development stages of childhood (Luke 2:52).
- He worked as a carpenter (Mark 6:3).
- He became hungry and thirsty (Matthew 4:2; John 19:28).
- He became tired and fatigued (Mark 4:38).
- He experienced sadness and sorrow (John 11:35).
- He became amazed (Matthew 8:10).
- He functioned with limited knowledge (Matthew 24:36).
- He became angry (Mark 11:15–16; John 2:13–17).
- He was apprehensive about his impending suffering (Matthew 26:38).
- His became disappointed (Matthew 26:40–45).
- He bled and died (John 19:33–34).

At Bethel Theological Seminary in San Diego, California, where Dr. Mark Strauss has been a professor of New Testament for more than a dozen years, we commandeered a classroom area off the library for our conversation about Jesus' real identity. Strauss is an unusual blend of academic acumen and an amiable and winsome personal style. His enthusiasm and quick wit make him popular in the classroom.

Strauss earned degrees in psychology, theology, and New Testament before spending four years at the University of Aberdeen in Scotland to get his doctorate in New Testament studies. He's the author of numerous books on technical and more popular topics, including *The Davidic Messiah in Luke-Acts: The Promise and Its Fulfillment in Lukan Christology*; *Distorting Scripture?: The Challenge of Bible Translation and Gender Accuracy*; *The Essential Bible Companion*; and the gospel of Luke section for *The Illustrated Bible Background Commentary*. In addition, he was a general editor and contributor, along with such other notable scholars as D. A. Carson and Douglas J. Moo, of *The Challenge of Bible Translation*. His most recent book is *Four Portraits, One Jesus: An Introduction to Jesus and the Gospels*.

While Strauss's scholarly interests are reflected in his memberships in the Society of Biblical Literature and the Institute for Biblical Research, he also dabbles in projects aimed at popular culture. He served, for instance, as technical editor of *The Complete Idiot's Guide to Mary Magdalene*—a project that exposed him to *The Da Vinci Code*.

I started our discussion by recapping *The Da Vinci Code*'s claims about Jesus, and then I read this quote attributed to Sir Leigh Teabing: "Many scholars claim that the early Church literally *stole* Jesus from his original followers, hijacking his human message, shrouding it in an impenetrable cloak of divinity, and using it to expand their own power."

"How much of that," I asked Strauss, "is truth and how much of it is fiction?"

"That's an extraordinary statement of revisionist history," was his response. "In fact, when I was reading *The Da Vinci Code*, I was quite enjoying it as a fascinating murder mystery. Each chapter leaves you hanging and you can't put it down. But when I got to the chapter on Jesus' deity, suddenly it spoiled the whole book for me. Because what we have in that chapter is two supposed historical experts suddenly spouting absolute historical nonsense—stuff that any historian could tell you is pure gibberish."

That was worth unpacking. "So 325 AD was not the first time that Jesus was declared deity?"

"Absolutely not. The Council of Nicea of 325 was extraordinarily important. The conversion of Constantine, the first emperor to become a Christian, was enormously important for the church. It freed up the church from having to suffer persecution," Strauss said.

"But the idea that Constantine at the Council of Nicea made Jesus into a deity from a mere mortal prophet is ridiculous. The church had been declaring Jesus' deity for more than two hundred and fifty years. In fact, to determine when the church is speaking about Jesus' deity, simply go to the New Testament. More than two hundred and fifty years earlier, we get statement after statement that, in fact, affirm Jesus' deity in the New Testament documents themselves."

"Well, Dan Brown would challenge you on that," I pointed out, "because he also makes the assertion that Constantine took Matthew, Mark, Luke, and John, which describe the deity of Jesus, and he embellished those. Then he took the gospels that said Jesus was merely a human being, and he had those destroyed. Could it be true that there are some destroyed or missing gospels that make it clear that Jesus is just a human being?"

For a scholar like Strauss, this simply didn't make sense. "That claim completely convolutes history," he said. "Dan Brown suggests that there were eighty or so gospels whirling around and the church just chose those particular gospels which they viewed as authoritative, supporting their particular perspective. That just runs absolutely contrary to what we know about the historical facts.

"The four Gospels from the New Testament, what we call the canonical Gospels, are the only historical documents that really can be shown, with certainty, to be first-century documents. That is, they are documents that arose within the first and second generation of Jesus' followers. The claim that these other gospels were competing with those until this particular date is just simply not accurate."

The Claims of Jesus

I asked, "If the New Testament Gospels are the most reliable documents we have, does Jesus, in these Gospels, come right out and make the claim that he is God?"

"Absolutely, Jesus makes the claim that he is God," Strauss said. "In chapter 8 of John's gospel, Jesus is in a dialogue with his Jewish opponents, and they claim Abraham is their father. Jesus responds by saying, "Before Abraham was, I Am"—which is kind of a strange response.

"But what is obvious from that response is that Jesus is, in fact, referring to chapter 3 of Exodus in the Old Testament, where God reveals himself to Moses as the 'I Am.' It's a clear claim to deity and a claim to preexistence. It's a claim to being the Creator of the universe. Now, we know that's exactly what he meant, because the immediate response from his opponents is that they pick up stones to stone him to death. They immediately recognize that Jesus is claiming to be God, and they accuse him of blasphemy and attempt to kill him.

"In John 10, Jesus says, 'I and the Father are one.' Again, this is a clear reference to his deity. In John 14, Philip comes to Jesus and he says, 'Jesus, show us the Father.' And Jesus responds, 'Have you been with me so long and you don't yet get it?' He says, 'He who has seen me has seen the Father.' Again, Jesus claims to be one and the same with God the Father."

"So, Jesus understood that he was making a claim to deity?"

"Yes, without question, this is who he thought he was. He understood that this was an incredibly exalted claim, that he was claiming deity," replied Strauss. "And he was also claiming that he would be the one to judge human beings. This is another astonishing statement of authority. Throughout the Gospels, Jesus claims that he is the one who would decide the eternal fate of human beings. He claims to be the final judge. Well, from a biblical perspective, that can be no one else but God, because God is the final judge of all people."

I decided to approach the issue another way. "Do you see any place," I asked, "where Jesus *denies* that he is the Son of God?"

"He had plenty of opportunities to deny this part of his identity, because over and over again it got him in trouble, particularly when the religious leaders began picking up stones to stone him," Strauss said. "Jesus could have easily said, 'Hold on just a minute! You've completely misunderstood me. Let me explain what I really meant.' But nowhere does he do that."

"In other words," I said, "he had the opportunity to deny his identity, but he didn't take it?"

Declared Strauss: "Absolutely."

3. *The Da Vinci Code* says that Christianity as we know it today is essentially the work, not of Jesus and his disciples, but of the Emperor Constantine, who reigned over the Roman Empire in the fourth century. To what extent do you think this is true or false? Explain.

4. According to the following biblical references, to what extent do you think Jesus claimed to be God? Explain.

- Jesus claimed he would judge the world at the end of time (Matthew 7:21–23; John 5:22).
- Jesus claimed he should be honored as much as God (John 5:23).
- Jesus claimed he could impart eternal life to people (John 5:21, 40).
- Jesus claimed that to see him was to see God (John 14:9).
- Jesus claimed that to know him was to know God (John 8:19).
- Jesus claimed that to hate him was to hate God (John 15:23).
- Jesus claimed he could forgive sin (Mark 2:5, 10).
- Jesus accepted worship and being called "God" (John 20:28–29).
- Jesus claimed titles exclusive to God (John 8:56–58).
- Jesus claimed he and the Father are one (John 10:22–33).
- Jesus claimed he had been with God in heaven and shared divine glory (John 17:5).

- Jesus claimed he could hear and answer prayers (John 14:14).
- After the resurrection, Jesus claimed he was omnipresent (Matthew 28:20; John 14:23).

5. Do you know of any example when Jesus attempted to deny his divinity? If Jesus didn't want us to conclude he was God, how could he have made that clear?

With the identity of Jesus being such a core issue to both Christianity and *The Da Vinci Code*, there were still several areas of inquiry I wanted to pursue with Strauss. I resumed our dialogue with this question: "What did the earliest followers of Jesus believe about his identity?"

Explained Strauss: "One of the most indisputable facts about early Christianity was that very shortly after Jesus' crucifixion, his followers began to proclaim that he was the Son of God, risen from the dead, exalted to the right hand of the Father. Read through the book of Acts and you see that his followers are praying to and worshiping Jesus.

"Now, in our Christian context, that may not be so surprising. But place that prayer and worship in the context of first-century Judaism, which is thoroughly monotheistic and believes in only one true God of Israel, then all of a sudden you have a shocking thing going on. Jewish Christians, in first-century Israel, praying to Jesus as God—now that's *really* shocking."

Obviously, those followers of Jesus needed more than just his claim that he was divine; certainly, they must have required some sort of proof to prompt their worship of him. "What evidence is there to really support his claim and back it up?" I asked. "What credentials does Jesus offer to convince us?"

Strauss could have mentioned several strands of evidence, including Jesus' miracles and fulfillment of ancient prophecies. Instead, he said, "I think the greatest and final evidence, as Jesus himself said, is his resurrection from the dead. He made extraordinary claims about himself, and then he predicted that he would rise from the dead. Everything he said could have been disproved if the resurrection hadn't happened. But, in fact, it happened—and the evidence for the resurrection is really extraordinary."

"You believe that the resurrection of Jesus Christ is the ultimate authentication of his claim to being the Son of God?" I asked.

"Absolutely," he responded. "And I think the historical evidence for the resurrection is really overwhelming, even when you approach it from a skeptic's perspective."

An interesting comment, I mused—especially since he was talking with a former atheist. But before I could ask him to spell out the evidence, he continued by saying, "Here are just five basic, almost indisputable historical facts related to the resurrection. The first is that Jesus actually died on the cross. The Romans made sure he really died. Second, he was buried in a tomb. In fact, we have the name of the owner of the tomb: Joseph of Arimathea.

"Third, not only was he buried, but three days later the tomb was empty. Jesus' opponents never claimed that the tomb wasn't empty. They could have gone and gotten the body and shown the body to prove that he hadn't risen from the dead. Instead, they said that the disciples stole the body. So, the tomb was, in fact, empty.

"Fourth, Jesus' followers saw him alive again, and they were willing to die for that claim. And, finally, the disciples' lives were absolutely transformed through faith in Christ. These people were willing, in Jerusalem, to proclaim the death, burial, and resurrection of Jesus, even though they faced almost certain death."

There it was: in five pithy points, Strauss had outlined a persuasive case for Jesus rising from the dead. Entire books have been written to elaborate on these basic facts, but even this brief summary was enough to communicate the power of the evidence.

"If you were on a jury, weighing this evidence," I asked, "you would render the verdict that Jesus really must be who he claimed to be?"

Strauss was quick to reply. "Yes, I think the evidence is overwhelming," he said. "I would say, 'Yes, absolutely, Jesus was who he claimed to be, the Son of God; God in flesh.'"

What to Do Now?

I could have ended the interview there, but there was something bothering me. Some people, I said to Strauss, find the idea that God came and lived among us to be very positive and hopeful. For others, though, it generates hostility. They seem to get angry at the very idea. "Why," I asked, "does the claim that Jesus is the unique Son of God spark so much opposition?"

As I suspected he would, Strauss gave a thoughtful answer. "I think there are various reasons," he began. "One is that there is some difficulty in the logic of it. For us to try to conceive of what it would be like to be both human and divine is very difficult to think about, and so people have struggled with that idea. And they try to solve the mystery of the incarnation by coming down on one of two sides, either denying Jesus' deity, on the one hand, or denying his humanity.

"Those who deny his humanity claim that Jesus wasn't truly a human being. He only appeared to be a human being—that's called Docetism, from a Greek word meaning "to appear" or "to seem like." Those who deny his deity claim that he was really just a mere human being, a good prophet and a good man, but not God. They would claim that Jesus was a very powerful individual in a lot of different ways, but that his followers later turned him into a god. And so there are those attempts to solve the logic.

"I think another reason is, we are, by nature, fallen human beings and in rebellion against God, and to acknowledge that Jesus is, in fact, truly human and truly

God means that he has certain claims on our lives—and we don't really want to submit to those claims. We don't want to depend on him for our salvation, because it means we have to let go. Jesus said, 'If anyone wants to follow me, they have to deny themselves, take up their cross and follow me.' That means we have to give up our own lives and give ourselves fully to him. And by nature, this isn't easy to do."

"Well, Dr. Strauss, if it is true that Jesus is the Son of God, then what are the implications for all of us living in the twenty-first century? What does it mean for us today?"

"These are really the fundamental questions of life. Every human being looks at the world and says, 'Why am I here? Is there a purpose and meaning for my life? Where am I going?' Well, if Jesus is who he said he was—the Son of God, who came to earth to reverse the effects of our fallen human nature—then *he* is the answer to the ultimate questions of life.

"Every person," he concluded, "needs to settle these questions. If Jesus is indeed truly God, who suffered and died for my sins, then I need to respond to him by faith. I need to trust him as my personal Forgiver and Leader."

6. According to Mark Strauss, who did Jesus' earliest followers think he was? Do you agree with Strauss' perspective? Why or why not?

Considered Divine Before AD 325?

Long before the Council of Nicaea, people considered Jesus divine:

- Ignatius: "God Himself was manifested in human form" (AD 105).
- Clement: "It is fitting that you should think of Jesus Christ as of God" (AD 150).
- Justin Martyr: "Being the first-begotten Word of God, is even God"; "Both God and Lord of hosts"; "The Father of the universe has a Son. And He ... is even God" (AD 160).
- Irenaeus: "Our Lord, and God, and Savior, and King"; "He is God, for the name Emmanuel indicates this" (AD 180).
- Tertullian: "Christ our God" (AD 200).
- Origen: "No one should be offended that the Savior is also God" (AD 225).
- Novatian: "He is not only man, but God also" (AD 235).
- Cyprian: "Jesus Christ, our Lord and God" (AD 250).
- Methodius: "He truly was and is ... with God, and being God" (AD 290).
- Lactantius: "We believe Him to be God" (AD 304).
- Arnobius: "Christ performed all these miracles ... the duty of Divinity" (AD 305).

James Garlow and Peter Jones
In *Cracking Da Vinci's Code*

7. Anyone can claim to be God, but Jesus actually convinced his followers that he was telling the truth about his divine identity by:

- Performing miracles (even the Jewish Talmud and the Islamic Koran concede he worked the supernatural).
- Living a sinless life (two of his closest companions, John and Peter, report his moral perfection; see 1 John 3:5 and 1 Peter 2:22).
- Fulfilling ancient messianic prophecies against all mathematical odds.
- Resurrecting from the dead.

Do you believe these arguments provide convincing evidence that Jesus was God incarnate? Why or why not?

8. If Jesus really is the Son of God, then why would he have chosen to enter into human history, only to be tortured to death in the end? What would it take to have motivated you, if you were God, to do the same thing?

Clear in Word and Deed?

"Jesus made it clear by word and deed that to know him was to know God, to see him was to see God, to believe in him was to believe in God, to receive him was to receive God, to reject him was to reject God, and to honor him was to honor God."

British pastor John Stott

9. Some people find the idea that God came and lived among us very exciting and hopeful. Yet, history shows a widespread hostility to this belief. Why do you think his deity sparks such opposition?

Faith in Jesus?

"Modern Christianity may certainly be diverse, but at the core of all Christian faith is the belief that Jesus, fully divine and fully human, is the One through whom God reconciled the world — and each one of us — to Himself, and that salvation is found through faith in Jesus, who is not dead but lives."
Amy Welborn in *De-Coding Da Vinci*

10. What aspect of Jesus' divinity is difficult or troublesome for you to accept? Why?

11. If it is true that Jesus really is God in the flesh, what are some implications for *your* life today?

A Great Human Teacher?

"Either this man was, and is, the Son of God: or else a madman or something worse. You can shut him up for a fool, you can spit at him and kill him as a demon; or you can fall at his feet and call him Lord and God. But let us not come with any patronizing nonsense about him being a great human teacher. He has not left that open to us. He did not intend to."

C. S. Lewis

12. The disciple Thomas had doubts about Jesus until he saw him resurrected in person and said, "My Lord and my God!" (see John 20:24–31). What do you think it would take (or what did it take) for you to draw the same conclusion about Jesus?

As I braced myself against a biting wind and looked up at the western façade of Westminster Abbey, its twin towers rising 225 feet into the air between a shield of stained glass, it was difficult for me to believe that this stunning masterpiece of thirteenth- to sixteenth-century architecture is also a colossal cemetery.

Yet buried around the Abbey are the remains of three thousand people, including such notables as St. Edward the Confessor, the last of the Anglo-Saxon kings; scientists Sir Isaac Newton and Charles Darwin; poets and authors Robert Browning, Geoffrey Chaucer, Charles Dickens, Thomas Hardy, Rudyard Kipling, and Alfred

Tennyson; the adventurer David Livingstone; and the father-son prime ministers of England, William Pitt, First Earl of Chatham, and William Pitt the Younger.

Soaking in the ambience at this pivotal *Da Vinci Code* site, I began to muse about how the novel and movie might have turned out differently. What if, for instance, during the climactic scene that took place in the Abbey, one of these graves slowly opened up and Sir Isaac Newton, supposedly a long-ago Grand Master of the Priory of Sion, stepped forth—alive—to intervene in the conflict? It would have been a highly dramatic but totally absurd plot twist—why? Because nobody would have believed it. Dead people don't come back to life.

Christianity, though, is based on the premise that Jesus *did* overcome the grave. And it was the compelling historical evidence for the resurrection that prompted me on November 8, 1981, to abandon my atheism and become a follower of Christ. After all, anyone can claim to be the Son of God, as Jesus repeatedly did, even in the earliest gospel of all, the gospel of Mark. It's quite another thing to back it up by returning from the dead. But the evidence was strong enough to convince even a skeptic like me.

As Strauss said, everybody in the ancient world agreed Jesus' tomb was empty. His opponents made up the absurd story that the disciples had stolen his body, but they lacked both motive and opportunity. What's more, Jesus appeared alive to more than 515 eyewitnesses, including skeptics whose lives were revolutionized as a result. The report of his resurrection comes so soon after the event that it simply cannot be the product of legendary development. Finally, there's the willingness of the disciples to die for their conviction that Jesus had returned to life. They didn't just *believe* the resurrection was true; they were in a unique position to *know* first-hand that it had actually occurred. Nobody knowingly and willingly dies for a lie.

Compared to the avalanche of evidence for the truth of Christianity, Dan Brown offers nothing with any credibility to support his historical revisionism. *The Da Vinci Code* is a creative romp that has captured the imaginations of millions of people. Give Brown credit for being one of the most successful novelists of all time, but there is simply no rational reason to believe his book's audacious rewriting of Christianity.

In sharp contrast, I believe that the verdict of history is clear: Jesus is who he claimed to be—the one and only Son of God and Savior of the world. The one who I asked to become my Forgiver and Leader nearly twenty-five years ago, and who since then has revolutionized my life for the better.

So that leaves you. Maybe, like following the riddles and codes in Dan Brown's adventure story, you need to pursue more clues about the identity of Jesus. If that's the case, then you should be encouraged that both the Old and New Testaments promise that those who look for the true God will, indeed, find him.

Maybe the best way to start is to follow Scot McKnight's suggestion—read the Gospels, perhaps starting with the one written by Luke, who "carefully investigated everything" so he could write "an orderly account" about "the certainty" of what took place. I hope you'll keep an open mind and promise yourself at the outset that you'll reach a verdict when the evidence is in. You might even want to whisper a prayer to the God you're not sure exists, asking him to lead you to the truth about him.

After all, there's a lot riding on your verdict. If Jesus really is the Son of God, then your eternity hinges on how you respond to him. As Jesus said in John 8:24, "If you do not believe that I am the one I claim to be, you will indeed die in your sins."

Those are sober words, offered out of loving concern. In fact, his love for you is so great that he willingly suffered the agony of the cross to pay the penalty for all the wrong things you've ever done. He offers complete forgiveness, his leadership and guidance, and an open door to heaven to all who put their trust in him.

You've probably heard that the catch phrase for *The Da Vinci Code* movie is, "Seek the truth." That's good advice, but frankly, I like the way Jesus put it in Luke 7: "So I say to you: Ask and it will be given to you; seek and you will find; knock and the door will be opened to you."

Appendix 1

FOR FURTHER STUDY

Blomberg, Craig. *The Historical Reliability of the Gospels*. Downers Grove, Ill.: InterVarsity Press, 1987.

Bruce, F. F. *The New Testament Documents: Are They Reliable?* Grand Rapids, Mich.: Eerdmans, 2003.

Copan, Paul, ed. *Will the Real Jesus Please Stand Up? A Debate Between William Lane Craig and John Dominic Crossan*. Grand Rapids, Mich.: Baker, 1998.

Habermas, Gary. *The Historical Jesus*. Joplin, Mo.: College Press, 1996.

Metzger, Bruce. *The Canon of the New Testament*. London: Oxford University Press, 1997.

Patzia, Arthur G. *The Making of the New Testament: Origin, Collection, Text and Canon*. Downers Grove, Ill.: InterVarsity Press, 1995.

Strobel, Lee. *The Case for Christ*. Grand Rapids, Mich.: Zondervan, 1998. Also available in student edition.

Wilkins, Michael J. and J. P. Moreland, eds. *Jesus Under Fire*. Grand Rapids, Mich.: Zondervan, 1995.

Appendix 2

FAQS ABOUT THE DA VINCI CODE

Mark L. Strauss, PhD
Bethel Seminary San Diego

The Da Vinci Code *claims:*

- Almost everything the church teaches about Jesus is false.
- Jesus was only human. No one claimed he was divine until a church council in the fourth century declared him to be a god.
- Jesus was married to Mary Magdalene.
- Mary was pregnant when Jesus was crucified.
- Their offspring are alive today, a secret kept by the Priory of Sion.
- Mary herself is the "Holy Grail."
- Mary appears in Leonardo Da Vinci's *The Last Supper*.
- Earliest Christianity worshiped the divine feminine. The later church suppressed this.
- The Gospels (Matthew, Mark, Luke, and John) are just four among eighty or so other gospels. These other gospels, which described Jesus' relationship to Mary, were suppressed by the church. History, says author Dan Brown, is written by the winners.

Was Jesus' deity created by the church in the fourth century?

- The Council of Nicea in AD 325 debated important issues, and confirmed Jesus' deity. But it did not create it. Christians had been worshiping Jesus and proclaiming his deity for centuries.
- The New Testament already explicitly claims Jesus' deity. (See, for example, John 1:1; Colossians 1:15; Hebrews 1:3.)

Who was Mary Magdalene?

There are many legends, only a few certainties:

- One of the women who supported Jesus (Luke 8:1–3).
- A recipient of Jesus' exorcism (Luke 8:2).
- The first witness to the resurrection (John 20:10–18).
- Not a prostitute and unlikely the woman caught in adultery (John 8:1–11).

Was Jesus married to Mary Magdalene?

- Though Jewish men of Jesus' day were usually married, there were many exceptions. For example:
  - The Essenes of the Dead Sea community at Qumran remained single.
  - The apostle Paul was single (1 Corinthians 7:7).
  - In both Judaism and Christianity, singleness and celibacy were esteemed as a means to complete devotion to the Lord (1 Corinthians 7:32–33).
  - While most rabbis were married, Jesus more closely fulfilled the role of a prophet. Prophets often remained single to be wholly devoted to the Lord.
  - John the Baptist, the prophet and forerunner of the Messiah, was unmarried.
- All of the evidence indicates Jesus was single.
  - Jesus said the Son of Man had no place to lay his head (Matthew 8:20; Luke 9:58).

- From the cross, Jesus commends his mother to John's care, but does not mention a wife.
- There is no hint of any sexual or marital relationship between Jesus and the women who supported him.

- There is not a shred of early or reliable historical evidence that Jesus was married.

Does Mary Magdalene appear in Da Vinci's Last Supper?

- Art historians recognize this as John the apostle, not Mary Magdalene.
- John the apostle is not seen elsewhere in the painting.
- John is often depicted in art as a young, feminine-looking man.
- In early sketches, Da Vinci himself identified this as John, not Mary.

Were the four Gospels of the Bible arbitrarily chosen from among more than eighty contenders?

- The New Testament Gospels are by far the oldest and most reliable records we have of the historical Jesus.
- The so-called "apocryphal gospels" were written decades (most, centuries) after the New Testament Gospels.
- The vast majority of "apocryphal gospels" are very late, fanciful, and dependent on the four Gospels.
- The few outside sources we have confirm the picture of Jesus found in the Gospels (see Josephus, *Antiquities* 18.3.3 §§63–64).

Is the Bible a merely human book?

- It is true that the Bible did not drop from heaven. No scholar claims it did.
- The Bible claims to be inspired by God, with human authors communicating God's message.

- Translations today come from very early Greek and Hebrew manuscripts (not "countless" versions).
- We have extraordinarily reliable manuscripts, very close to the originals.
- The divine origin of the Bible is confirmed by fulfilled prophecy and its transforming power.

Did the pagan Roman emperor Constantine choose which books to put in the Bible?

- Constantine converted to Christianity, so he was not a "pagan" emperor.
- Constantine had nothing to do with which books were included in the Bible.
- The New Testament books were considered inspired Scripture long before Constantine was born.

Are the Dead Sea Scrolls "lost gospels"?

- The Dead Sea Scrolls are Jewish, not Christian writings, written a hundred-plus years before Jesus was born. They have nothing to do with him.
- Jesus is (of course) never mentioned in the scrolls.

Are the Gnostic gospels the earliest Christian records?

- Almost all scholars date the Gnostic gospels to the second century or later, and consider them to be dependent on the four New Testament Gospels. They are certainly not the earliest Christian records.
- The suggestion that Jesus was originally a Gnostic does not fit his historical context. Jesus was a first-century Palestinian Jew (everyone agrees on this), and his earliest followers were Palestinian Jews. The New Testament Gospels place Jesus accurately in this first-century Jewish context.

- The Gnostic literature does not fit this historical background, suggesting that it was a later development that arose under the influence of Greek philosophical thought.

Does the Gnostic Gospel of Philip reveal Jesus' marital relationship with Mary Magdalene?

- The *Gospel of Philip* is dated to the third century AD and has no legitimate claim to authenticity.
- The identification of Mary as Jesus' companion is part of a Gnostic worldview that spirit beings exist in male and female forms.

Was the early church misogynist and did it suppress women?

- Jesus highly valued women, raising them to the position of disciples or close followers (consider Mary and Martha in Luke 10:38–42). A group of women supported his ministry.
- Women receive a higher place in the church than in the pagan world or in Judaism (see Lydia, Priscilla, Phoebe, and Junia).
- Pagan goddess worship generally "used" women. It did not exalt them.
- The Gnostic documents themselves are misogynist. For example, in the *Gospel of Thomas*, Jesus says of Mary, "I myself shall lead her in order to make her male.... For every woman who will make herself male will enter the Kingdom of Heaven."

Has Jesus' royal bloodline (through Mary Magdalene) been documented by many reputable historians?

- This "historical fact" has no validity and is not supported by any real historians.
- It has been promoted in the book, *Holy Blood, Holy Grail*, by Michael Baigent, Richard Leigh, and Henry Lincoln, none of whom are historians or scholars.

Do Christian symbols have pagan origins?

- It is certainly true that Christians took over pagan symbols and "baptized" them with Christian meaning.
- The real question is: Is the new meaning Christian or pagan?

Was Sunday worship started by Constantine as part of the worship of the sun?

- This is false. The New Testament shows Christians worshiping on the first day of the week (Sunday) during the first century (Acts 20:7; 1 Corinthians 16:2; Revelation 1:10).
- Christians worshiped on Sunday because it was the day of the resurrection.

EVIDENCE FOR THE TRUE IDENTITY OF JESUS

Lee Strobel

The Da Vinci Code paints Jesus as being a mere human being who was turned into a god almost three hundred years after his death by Emperor Constantine for the ruler's own selfish purposes. However, that's not what I discovered during my own spiritual investigation into Jesus' identity. As an atheist, I spent two years checking out Jesus and coming to the conclusion that he is the unique Son of God. Here is a summary of the historical evidence for Jesus Christ from thirteen leading experts who were interviewed for my book *The Case for Christ*:

Can the biographies of Jesus be trusted?

I once thought that the Gospels were merely religious propaganda, hopelessly tainted by overactive imaginations and evangelistic zeal. But Craig Blomberg of Denver Seminary, one of the country's foremost authorities on the biographies of Jesus, built a convincing case that they reflect eyewitness testimony and bear the unmistakable earmarks of accuracy. So early are these accounts of Jesus' life that they cannot be explained away as legendary inventions. "Within the first two years after his death," Blomberg said, "significant numbers of Jesus' followers seem to have formulated a doctrine of the atonement, were convinced that he had been raised from the dead in bodily form, associated Jesus with God, and believed they found support for all these convictions in the Old Testament." A study indicates that there was nowhere near enough time for legend to have developed and wiped out a solid core of historical truth.

Do Jesus' biographies stand up to scrutiny?

Blomberg argued persuasively that the Gospel writers intended to preserve reliable history; were able to do so; were honest and willing to include difficult-to-explain material; and didn't allow bias to unduly color their reporting. The harmony among the Gospels on essential facts, coupled with divergence on some incidental details, lends historical credibility to the accounts. What's more, the early church could not have taken root and flourished right there in Jerusalem if it had been teaching facts about Jesus that his own contemporaries could have exposed as exaggerated or false. In short, the Gospels were able to pass all eight evidential tests, demonstrating their basic trustworthiness as historical records.

Were Jesus' biographies reliably preserved for us?

World-class scholar Bruce Metzger, professor emeritus at Princeton Theological Seminary, said that compared to other ancient documents, there is an unprecedented number of New Testament manuscripts and that they can be dated extremely close to the original writings. The modern New Testament is 99.5 percent free of textual discrepancies, with no major Christian doctrine in doubt. The criteria used by the early church to determine which books should be considered authoritative have ensured that we possess the best records about Jesus.

Is there credible evidence for Jesus outside his biographies?

"We have better historical documentation for Jesus than for the founder of any other ancient religion," said Edwin Yamauchi of Miami University, a leading expert on ancient history. Sources from outside the Bible corroborate that many people believed Jesus performed healings and was the Messiah; that he was crucified; and that despite this shameful death, his followers, who believed he was still alive, worshiped him as God. One expert documented thirty-nine ancient sources that corroborate more than one hundred facts concerning Jesus' life, teachings, crucifixion, and resurrection. Seven secular sources and several early Christian creeds concern the deity of Jesus, a doctrine "definitely present in the earliest church," according to Dr. Gary Habermas, the scholar who wrote *The Historical Jesus*.

Does archaeology confirm or contradict Jesus' biographies?

John McRay, a professor of archaeology for more than fifteen years and author of *Archaeology and the New Testament*, said there's no question that archaeological findings have enhanced the New Testament's credibility. No discovery has ever disproved a biblical reference. Further, archaeology has established that Luke, who wrote about one-quarter of the New Testament, was an especially careful historian. Concluded one expert: "If Luke was so painstakingly accurate in his historical reporting [of minor details], on what logical basis may we assume he was credulous or inaccurate in his reporting of matters that were far more important, not only to him but to others as well?" Like, for instance, the resurrection of Jesus—the event that authenticated his claim to being the unique Son of God.

Is the Jesus of history the same as the Jesus of faith?

Gregory Boyd, a Yale- and Princeton-educated scholar who wrote the award-winning *Cynic Sage or Son of God?*, offered a devastating critique of the Jesus Seminar, a group that questions whether Jesus said or did most of what's attributed to him. He identified the Seminar as "an extremely small number of radical-fringe scholars who are on the far, far left wing of New Testament thinking." The Seminar ruled out the possibility of miracles at the outset, employed questionable criteria, and some participants have touted myth-riddled documents of extremely dubious quality. Further, the idea that stories about Jesus emerged from mythology fails to withstand scrutiny. In sum, the Jesus of faith is the same as the Jesus of history.

Was Jesus really convinced he was the Son of God?

By going back to the very earliest traditions, which were unquestionably safe from legendary development, Ben Witherington III, author of *The Christology of Jesus*, was able to show that Jesus had a supreme and transcendent self-understanding. Based on the evidence, Witherington said: "Did Jesus believe he was the Son of God, the anointed one of God? The answer is yes. Did he see himself as the Son of Man? The answer is yes. Did he see himself as the final Messiah? Yes, that's the way he viewed himself. Did he believe that anybody less than God could save the world? No, I don't believe he did." Scholars said that Jesus' repeated reference to himself as the Son of Man was not a claim of humanity, but a reference to Daniel 7:13–14, in which the Son of Man is seen as having universal authority and everlasting dominion and who receives the worship of all nations. Said one scholar: "Thus, the claim to be the Son of Man would be in effect a claim to divinity."

Was Jesus crazy when he claimed to be the Son of God?

Gary Collins, a professor of psychology for twenty years and author of forty-five books on psychology-related topics, said Jesus exhibited no inappropriate emotions; was in contact with reality; was brilliant and had amazing insights into human nature; and enjoyed deep and abiding relationships. "I just don't see signs that Jesus was suffering from any known mental illness," he concluded. In addition, Jesus backed up his claim to being God through miraculous feats of healing; astounding demonstrations of power over nature; unrivaled teaching; divine understanding of people; and with his own resurrection, which was the ultimate evidence of his deity.

Did Jesus fulfill the attributes of God?

While the incarnation—God becoming man, the infinite becoming finite—stretches our imaginations, prominent theologian D. A. Carson pointed out that there's lots of evidence that Jesus exhibited the characteristics of deity. Based on Philippians 2, many theologians believe Jesus voluntarily emptied himself of the independent use of his divine attributes as he pursued his mission of human redemption. Even so, the New Testament specifically confirms that Jesus ultimately possessed every qualification of deity, including omniscience, omnipresence, omnipotence, eternality, and immutability.

Did Jesus—and Jesus alone—match the identity of the Messiah?

Hundreds of years before Jesus was born, prophets foretold the coming of the Messiah, or the Anointed One, who would redeem God's people. In effect, dozens of these Old Testament prophecies created a fingerprint that only the true Messiah could fit. This gave Israel a way to rule out imposters and validate the credentials of the authentic Messiah. Against astronomical odds—by one estimate, one chance in a trillion, trillion, trillion, trillion, trillion, trillion, trillion, trillion, trillion, trillion, trillion, trillion—Jesus, and only Jesus throughout history, matched this prophetic fingerprint. This confirms Jesus' identity to an incredible degree of certainty. The expert I interviewed on this topic, Louis Lapides, is an example of someone raised in a conservative Jewish home who came to believe Jesus is the Messiah after a systematic study of the prophecies. Today, he's a pastor of a church in California and former president of a national network of fifteen messianic congregations.

Was Jesus' death a sham, and his resurrection a hoax?

By analyzing the medical and historical data, Dr. Alexander Metherell, a physician who also holds a doctorate in engineering, concluded Jesus could not have survived the gruesome rigors of crucifixion, much less the gaping wound that pierced his lung and heart. In fact, even before the crucifixion he was in serious to critical condition and suffering from hypovolemic shock as the result of a horrific flogging. The idea that he swooned on the cross and pretended to be dead lacks any evidential basis. Roman executioners were grimly efficient, knowing that they themselves would face death if any of their victims were to come down from the cross alive. Even if Jesus had somehow lived through the torture, his ghastly condition could never have inspired a worldwide movement based on the premise that he had gloriously triumphed over the grave.

Was Jesus' body really absent from his tomb?

William Lane Craig, who has earned two doctorates and written several books on the resurrection, presented striking evidence that the enduring symbol of Easter — the vacant tomb of Jesus — was a historical reality. The empty grave is reported or implied in extremely early sources — Mark's gospel and a creed in 1 Corinthians 15 — which date so close to the event that they could not possibly have been products of legend. The fact that the Gospels report that women discovered the empty tomb bolsters the story's authenticity, because women's testimony lacked credibility in the first century and thus there would have been no motive to report they found the empty tomb if it weren't true. The site of Jesus' tomb was known to Christians, Jews, and Romans, so it could have been checked by skeptics. In fact, nobody — not even the Roman authorities or Jewish leaders — ever claimed that the tomb still contained Jesus' body. Instead, they were forced to invent the absurd story that the disciples, despite having no motive or opportunity, had stolen the body — a theory that not even the most skeptical critic believes today.

Was Jesus seen alive after his death on the cross?

The evidence for the post-resurrection appearances of Jesus didn't develop gradually over the years as mythology distorted memories of his life. Rather, said renowned resurrection expert Gary Habermas, his resurrection was "the central proclamation of the early church from the very beginning." The ancient creed from 1 Corinthians 15 mentions specific individuals who encountered the risen Christ, and Paul, in effect, challenged first-century doubters to talk with these individuals personally to determine the truth of the matter for themselves. The book of Acts is littered with extremely early affirmations of Jesus' resurrection, while the Gospels describe numerous encounters in detail. Concluded British theologian Michael Green: "The appearances of Jesus are as well authenticated as anything in antiquity.... There can be no rational doubt that they occurred."

Are there any supporting facts that point toward the resurrection?

Professor J. P. Moreland presented circumstantial evidence that provided strong documentation for the resurrection. First, the disciples were in a unique position to know whether the resurrection happened, and they went to their deaths proclaiming it was true. Nobody knowingly and willingly dies for a lie. Second, apart from the resurrection, there's no good reason why such skeptics as Paul and James would have been converted and would have died for their faith. Third, within weeks of the crucifixion, thousands of Jews became convinced Jesus was the Son of God and began following him, abandoning key social practices that had critical sociological and religious importance for centuries. They believed they risked damnation if they were wrong. Fourth, the early sacraments of Communion and baptism affirmed Jesus' resurrection and deity. And fifth, the miraculous emergence of the church in the face of brutal Roman persecution "rips a great hole in history, a hole the size and shape of resurrection," as C. F. D. Moule put it.

Taken together, I concluded that this expert testimony constitutes compelling evidence that Jesus Christ was who he claimed to be—the one and only Son of God. For details that support this summary, as well as other evidence, please refer to *The Case for Christ*.

Faith Under Fire Series

Lee Strobel and Garry Poole

Using video clips from the popular PAX-TV program Faith Under Fire, this cutting-edge DVD curriculum features spirited discussions between well-respected Christians, people of other faiths, or people with no faith at all on important spiritual and social issues. Host Lee Strobel, best-selling author of *The Case for Christ*, *The Case for Faith*, and *The Case for a Creator*, provides additional comments to guide small group discussion.

> *Guests include:* Rick Warren, Randy Alcorn, William Lane Craig, J. P. Moreland, Hugh Hewitt, Henry Cloud, Ergun Caner, Stephen Meyer, Albert Mohler, and more.

Each volume contains a four-session DVD and leader's guide, and is intended to be used in conjunction with a corresponding participant's guide (sold separately).

Faith Under Fire™ 1:
Faith & Jesus
Four sessions on Jesus,
the resurrection, universalism,
and the supernatural
DVD: 0-310-26828-1
Participant's Guide: 0-310-26829-X

Faith Under Fire™ 2:
Faith & Facts
Four sessions on the Bible,
heaven, hell, and science
DVD: 0-310-26850-8
Participant's Guide: 0-310-26851-6

Faith Under Fire™ 3:
Tough Faith Questions
Four sessions on forgiveness,
pain and suffering, the Trinity,
and Islam
DVD: 0-310-26855-9
Participant's Guide: 0-310-26856-7

Faith Under Fire™ 4:
A New Kind of Faith
Four sessions on the relevance
of Christianity
DVD: 0-310-26859-1
Participant's Guide: 0-310-26860-5

Discussing the Da Vinci Code
Group Discussion Kit

Examining the Issues Raised
by the Book & Movie

Lee Strobel and Garry Poole

This complete resource kit, designed specifically for groups of all sizes, includes a four-session DVD (with additional DVD-ROM resources) featuring Lee Strobel and filmed on location in London, Paris, and California; one copy of the Group Discussion Guide; and one copy of *Exploring the Da Vinci Code*.

Additional copies of both the *Discussing the Da Vinci Code* Group Discussion Guide and *Exploring the Da Vinci Code* can be purchased separately.

Group Discussion Kit: 0-310-27263-7
Group Discussion Guide: 0-310-27265-3